四緑木星命

Four Green Life Star

Feng Shui Essentials: Xuan Kong Life Star
FOUR GREEN LIFE STAR

Copyright © 2011 by Joey Yap
All rights reserved worldwide.
First Edition July 2011

All intellectual property rights contained or in relation to this book belongs to Joey Yap.

No part of this book may be copied, used, subsumed, or exploited in fact, field of thought or general idea, by any other authors or persons, or be stored in a retrieval system, transmitted or reproduced in any way, including but not limited to digital copying and printing in any form whatsoever worldwide without the prior agreement and written permission of the author.

The author can be reached at:

Mastery Academy of Chinese Metaphysics Sdn. Bhd. (611143-A)
19-3, The Boulevard, Mid Valley City,
59200 Kuala Lumpur, Malaysia.
Tel   : +603-2284 8080
Fax   : +603-2284 1218
Website : www.masteryacademy.com

DISCLAIMER:

The author, Joey Yap and the publisher, JY Books Sdn Bhd, have made their best efforts to produce this high quality, informative and helpful book. They have verified the technical accuracy of the information and contents of this book. Any information pertaining to the events, occurrences, dates and other details relating to the person or persons, dead or alive, and to the companies have been verified to the best of their abilities based on information obtained or extracted from various websites, newspaper clippings and other public media. However, they make no representation or warranties of any kind with regard to the contents of this book and accept no liability of any kind for any losses or damages caused or alleged to be caused directly or indirectly from using the information contained herein.

Published by JY Books Sdn. Bhd. (659134-T)

Table of content:

1	**LIFE STAR REFERENCE TABLE**	7
2	**INTRODUCTION**	12
3	**YOUR XUAN KONG LIFE STAR**	23
	Basic Attributes	24
4	**YOUR FENG SHUI ESSENTIALS**	27
	Directions	29
	Taking the Direction using a Compass	33
	Favorable Directions	39
	Unfavorable Directions	49
	Bed Alignment Direction	58
	Best Floor	60
	Personal Grand Duke Direction	65
	Personal Clash Direction	71
	Flying Star Effects	76
5	**THE FIVE ELEMENT**	97

6	**CHARACTERISTICS OF STAR**	109
	The Good	111
	The Bad	117
7	**CAREER AND WEALTH**	123
	Characteristics at work	124
	Suitable Job Roles	128
	Career and Wealth Guide	132
8	**RELATIONSHIPS**	139
	Guide for Relationships	140
9	**HEALTH**	145
	Guide for Health	146
10	**COMPATIBILITY with OTHER LIFE STARS**	151

LIFE STAR REFERENCE TABLE

Year Pillar and Gua Number Reference Table for 1912 - 2055

Animal	Year of Birth			Gua Number for Male	Gua Number for Female	Year of Birth			Gua Number for Male	Gua Number for Female
Rat	1912	壬子 Ren Zi	Water Rat	7	8	1936	丙子 Bing Zi	Fire Rat	1	5
Ox	1913	癸丑 Gui Chou	Water Ox	6	9	1937	丁丑 Ding Chou	Fire Ox	9	6
Tiger	1914	甲寅 Jia Yin	Wood Tiger	5	1	1938	戊寅 Wu Yin	Earth Tiger	8	7
Rabbit	1915	乙卯 Yi Mao	Wood Rabbit	4	2	1939	己卯 Ji Mao	Earth Rabbit	7	8
Dragon	1916	丙辰 Bing Chen	Fire Dragon	3	3	1940	庚辰 Geng Chen	Metal Dragon	6	9
Snake	1917	丁巳 Ding Si	Fire Snake	2	4	1941	辛巳 Xin Si	Metal Snake	5	1
Horse	1918	戊午 Wu Wu	Earth Horse	1	5	1942	壬午 Ren Wu	Water Horse	4	2
Goat	1919	己未 Ji Wei	Earth Goat	9	6	1943	癸未 Gui Wei	Water Goat	3	3
Monkey	1920	庚申 Geng Shen	Metal Monkey	8	7	1944	甲申 Jia Shen	Wood Monkey	2	4
Rooster	1921	辛酉 Xin You	Metal Rooster	7	8	1945	乙酉 Yi You	Wood Rooster	1	5
Dog	1922	壬戌 Ren Xu	Water Dog	6	9	1946	丙戌 Bing Xu	Fire Dog	9	6
Pig	1923	癸亥 Gui Hai	Water Pig	5	1	1947	丁亥 Ding Hai	Fire Pig	8	7
Rat	1924	甲子 Jia Zi	Wood Rat	4	2	1948	戊子 Wu Zi	Earth Rat	7	8
Ox	1925	乙丑 Yi Chou	Wood Ox	3	3	1949	己丑 Ji Chou	Earth Ox	6	9
Tiger	1926	丙寅 Bing Yin	Fire Tiger	2	4	1950	庚寅 Geng Yin	Metal Tiger	5	1
Rabbit	1927	丁卯 Ding Mao	Fire Rabbit	1	5	1951	辛卯 Xin Mao	Metal Rabbit	4	2
Dragon	1928	戊辰 Wu Chen	Earth Dragon	9	6	1952	壬辰 Ren Chen	Water Dragon	3	3
Snake	1929	己巳 Ji Si	Earth Snake	8	7	1953	癸巳 Gui Si	Water Snake	2	4
Horse	1930	庚午 Geng Wu	Metal Horse	7	8	1954	甲午 Jia Wu	Wood Horse	1	5
Goat	1931	辛未 Xin Wei	Metal Goat	6	9	1955	乙未 Yi Wei	Wood Goat	9	6
Monkey	1932	壬申 Ren Shen	Water Monkey	5	1	1956	丙申 Bing Shen	Fire Monkey	8	7
Rooster	1933	癸酉 Gui You	Water Rooster	4	2	1957	丁酉 Ding You	Fire Rooster	7	8
Dog	1934	甲戌 Jia Xu	Wood Dog	3	3	1958	戊戌 Wu Xu	Earth Dog	6	9
Pig	1935	乙亥 Yi Hai	Wood Pig	2	4	1959	己亥 Ji Hai	Earth Pig	5	1

- Please note that the date for the Chinese Solar Year starts on Feb 4. This means that if you were born in Feb 2 of 2002, you belong to the previous year 2001.

Year Pillar and Gua Number Reference Table for 1912 - 2055

Animal	Year of Birth			Gua Number for Male	Gua Number for Female	Year of Birth			Gua Number for Male	Gua Number for Female
Rat	1960	庚子 Geng Zi	Metal Rat	4	2	1984	甲子 Jia Zi	Wood Rat	7	8
Ox	1961	辛丑 Xin Chou	Metal Ox	3	3	1985	乙丑 Yi Chou	Wood Ox	6	9
Tiger	1962	壬寅 Ren Yin	Water Tiger	2	4	1986	丙寅 Bing Yin	Fire Tiger	5	1
Rabbit	1963	癸卯 Gui Mao	Water Rabbit	1	5	1987	丁卯 Ding Mao	Fire Rabbit	4	2
Dragon	1964	甲辰 Jia Chen	Wood Dragon	9	6	1988	戊辰 Wu Chen	Earth Dragon	3	3
Snake	1965	乙巳 Yi Si	Wood Snake	8	7	1989	己巳 Ji Si	Earth Snake	2	4
Horse	1966	丙午 Bing Wu	Fire Horse	7	8	1990	庚午 Geng Wu	Metal Horse	1	5
Goat	1967	丁未 Ding Wei	Fire Goat	6	9	1991	辛未 Xin Wei	Metal Goat	9	6
Monkey	1968	戊申 Wu Shen	Earth Monkey	5	1	1992	壬申 Ren Shen	Water Monkey	8	7
Rooster	1969	己酉 Ji You	Earth Rooster	4	2	1993	癸酉 Gui You	Water Rooster	7	8
Dog	1970	庚戌 Geng Xu	Metal Dog	3	3	1994	甲戌 Jia Xu	Wood Dog	6	9
Pig	1971	辛亥 Xin Hai	Metal Pig	2	4	1995	乙亥 Yi Hai	Wood Pig	5	1
Rat	1972	壬子 Ren Zi	Water Rat	1	5	1996	丙子 Bing Zi	Fire Rat	4	2
Ox	1973	癸丑 Gui Chou	Water Ox	9	6	1997	丁丑 Ding Chou	Fire Ox	3	3
Tiger	1974	甲寅 Jia Yin	Wood Tiger	8	7	1998	戊寅 Wu Yin	Earth Tiger	2	4
Rabbit	1975	乙卯 Yi Mao	Wood Rabbit	7	8	1999	己卯 Ji Mao	Earth Rabbit	1	5
Dragon	1976	丙辰 Bing Chen	Fire Dragon	6	9	2000	庚辰 Geng Chen	Metal Dragon	9	6
Snake	1977	丁巳 Ding Si	Fire Snake	5	1	2001	辛巳 Xin Si	Metal Snake	8	7
Horse	1978	戊午 Wu Wu	Earth Horse	4	2	2002	壬午 Ren Wu	Water Horse	7	8
Goat	1979	己未 Ji Wei	Earth Goat	3	3	2003	癸未 Gui Wei	Water Goat	6	9
Monkey	1980	庚申 Geng Shen	Metal Monkey	2	4	2004	甲申 Jia Shen	Wood Monkey	5	1
Rooster	1981	辛酉 Xin You	Metal Rooster	1	5	2005	乙酉 Yi You	Wood Rooster	4	2
Dog	1982	壬戌 Ren Xu	Water Dog	9	6	2006	丙戌 Bing Xu	Fire Dog	3	3
Pig	1983	癸亥 Gui Hai	Water Pig	8	7	2007	丁亥 Ding Hai	Fire Pig	2	4

- Please note that the date for the Chinese Solar Year starts on Feb 4. This means that if you were born in Feb 2 of 2002, you belong to the previous year 2001.

Year Pillar and Gua Number Reference Table for 1912 - 2055

Animal	Year of Birth			Gua Number for Male	Gua Number for Female	Year of Birth			Gua Number for Male	Gua Number for Female
Rat	2008	戊子 Wu Zi	Earth Rat	1	5	2032	壬子 Ren Zi	Water Rat	4	2
Ox	2009	己丑 Ji Chou	Earth Ox	9	6	2033	癸丑 Gui Chou	Water Ox	3	3
Tiger	2010	庚寅 Geng Yin	Metal Tiger	8	7	2034	甲寅 Jia Yin	Wood Tiger	2	4
Rabbit	2011	辛卯 Xin Mao	Metal Rabbit	7	8	2035	乙卯 Yi Mao	Wood Rabbit	1	5
Dragon	2012	壬辰 Ren Chen	Water Dragon	6	9	2036	丙辰 Bing Chen	Fire Dragon	9	6
Snake	2013	癸巳 Gui Si	Water Snake	5	1	2037	丁巳 Ding Si	Fire Snake	8	7
Horse	2014	甲午 Jia Wu	Wood Horse	4	2	2038	戊午 Wu Wu	Earth Horse	7	8
Goat	2015	乙未 Yi Wei	Wood Goat	3	3	2039	己未 Ji Wei	Earth Goat	6	9
Monkey	2016	丙申 Bing Shen	Fire Monkey	2	4	2040	庚申 Geng Shen	Metal Monkey	5	1
Rooster	2017	丁酉 Ding You	Fire Rooster	1	5	2041	辛酉 Xin You	Metal Rooster	4	2
Dog	2018	戊戌 Wu Xu	Earth Dog	9	6	2042	壬戌 Ren Xu	Water Dog	3	3
Pig	2019	己亥 Ji Hai	Earth Pig	8	7	2043	癸亥 Gui Hai	Water Pig	2	4
Rat	2020	庚子 Geng Zi	Metal Rat	7	8	2044	甲子 Jia Zi	Wood Rat	1	5
Ox	2021	辛丑 Xin Chou	Metal Ox	6	9	2045	乙丑 Yi Chou	Wood Ox	9	6
Tiger	2022	壬寅 Ren Yin	Water Tiger	5	1	2046	丙寅 Bing Yin	Fire Tiger	8	7
Rabbit	2023	癸卯 Gui Mao	Water Rabbit	4	2	2047	丁卯 Ding Mao	Fire Rabbit	7	8
Dragon	2024	甲辰 Jia Chen	Wood Dragon	3	3	2048	戊辰 Wu Chen	Earth Dragon	6	9
Snake	2025	乙巳 Yi Si	Wood Snake	2	4	2049	己巳 Ji Si	Earth Snake	5	1
Horse	2026	丙午 Bing Wu	Fire Horse	1	5	2050	庚午 Geng Wu	Metal Horse	4	2
Goat	2027	丁未 Ding Wei	Fire Goat	9	6	2051	辛未 Xin Wei	Metal Goat	3	3
Monkey	2028	戊申 Wu Shen	Earth Monkey	8	7	2052	壬申 Ren Shen	Water Monkey	2	4
Rooster	2029	己酉 Ji You	Earth Rooster	7	8	2053	癸酉 Gui You	Water Rooster	1	5
Dog	2030	庚戌 Geng Xu	Metal Dog	6	9	2054	甲戌 Jia Xu	Wood Dog	9	6
Pig	2031	辛亥 Xin Hai	Metal Pig	5	1	2055	乙亥 Yi Hai	Wood Pig	8	7

- Please note that the date for the Chinese Solar Year starts on Feb 4. This means that if you were born in Feb 2 of 2002, you belong to the previous year 2001.

Xuan Kong Nine Life Star

To download your Four Green Life Star Reference Chart FREE go to

www.masteryacademy.com/regbook

Here is your unique code for access:

GBSN6014

Introduction

When all is said and done, Feng Shui is the study of how environments affect the people living within them. It can yield advice on which environments, at both a macro and micro level, are 'good' places or 'bad' places to live for given people at given times.

Xuan Kong is only one subsection of the study of Feng Shui and the Life Stars are only one component in the Xuan Kong Feng Shui system. This means that the study of Life Stars gives us only one piece of the overall Feng Shui puzzle but it is an important one!

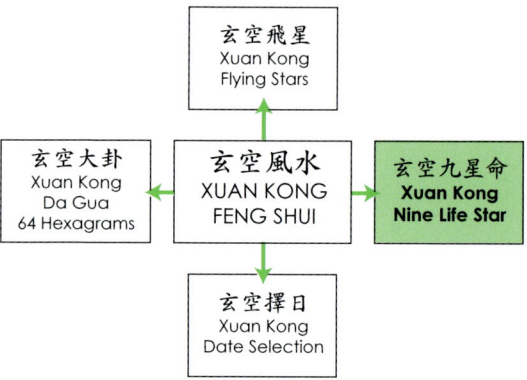

We can use the Xuan Kong Life Star system to help us with a number of practical Feng Shui and interpersonal decisions that make a big impact.

When we assess Feng Shui, we assess four factors: Environment, Buildings, Time and People. This book has been written to complement a number of other Feng Shui titles;

1. *Feng Shui for Homebuyers – Exterior;*
2. *Feng Shui for Homebuyers – Interior;*
3. *Feng Shui for Apartment Buyers;* and
4. *Pure Feng Shui.*

These other books talk about the influence of Environment, Buildings and Time on Feng Shui. This book looks at the final aspect: **People.**

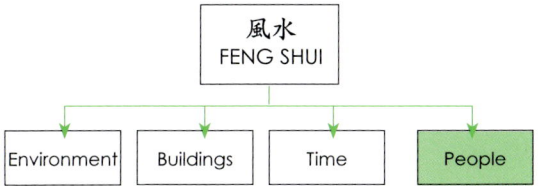

Different people will be affected in different ways by any given environment. The Life Stars directly determine what role the environment plays in the lives of its occupants. Every person is governed by one of the 9 Life Stars. These Stars also help determine key personal characteristics.

In this book, you will learn how the annually changing Xuan Kong Flying Stars interact with your Life Star so that you know what different sectors of your home will bring you. You can then use this information for your own benefit and safety. For maximum benefit, people should seek to align themselves with the direction in their home that yields positive effects. For instance, the #9 Purple Flying Star brings about the potential of career advancement for Star 1 people. Clearly this is a benefit that professionally minded people would like to take advantage of, so they may wish to spend more time absorbing the influence of the #9 Purple Flying Star in their home or place of work. The same Flying Star also indicates a heightened risk of miscarriage for pregnant women though and so pregnant Life Star 1 women should be exercise heightened caution in the presence of this Flying Star, and avoid its influence if possible.

Because the advice generated by this book on Xuan Kong Life Stars takes into account your Life Star when discussing the effects of the Flying Stars, the advice given is highly tailored to your life.

The Positive Side Of You

Your Life Star brings a force to bear on you, wherever you are. This force can have positive or negative effects, depending on the Feng Shui of the environment you reside in.

We are all multi faceted and complex. We have good habits and bad habits; a strong side and a weak side. By correctly tapping into the right Qi your best side will manifest itself more. When you put your best foot forward more in life, more opportunities

and success comes your way. Conversely, if you find yourself under the negative influence of your Life Star, more of your negative personality traits will prevail. Your environment filters out the good or the bad influence of your Life Star. Xuan Kong Feng Shui shows us how we can align ourself to receive the best possible influence. By simply aligning your bed and study desk to correspond with your favourable Personal Directions for example, you can already take one big step towards absorbing the beneficial influence of your Life Star, even whilst you sleep and study! If you are choosing a new home then choosing the correct floor at the correct time will bring further benefits. Avoiding your Personal Grand Duke and Crash Sectors will keep health problems and conflict at bay.

Does all of this mean you must tip-toe around certain rooms in your house or seal them off? No. Feng Shui does not need to become all consuming. If you can easily align your bed so that you receive benefits then why not do so? There are real world limits to what can be done, it is not practical, for instance, to rebuild your home if it does not perfectly cater to the instructions that this book gives. Your ideal floor choice in a condominium may not be available. The list of real world complications goes on.

You can tailor Feng Shui to work for you; making smaller, simple changes so that you reap the maximum possible benefit. The pursuit of good Feng Shui is not intended to take up all of your time and this flexible book is perfect for anyone, no matter how busy or restricted you are in your decisions.

Your Life Star

Everyone falls under the jurisdiction of one of the 9 Life Stars and this will have different consequences for everyone. Your Life Star describes your key skills, characteristics and traits. Some people are creative but reserved, some people are aggressive and driven. What self destructive traits do you have? Do you have a bloated sense of pride or are you prone to gossip? Your Life Star can shine some light on the complexity of your personality and your good and bad traits.

Study of the Life Stars has practical benefits for everyone; it gives you valuable information about others in addition to yourself. Different Life Stars bestow different abilities on people which means that people belonging to each Star will exhibit different characteristics at work. A Star 1 person is diplomatic so they are best suited to roles demanding diplomacy, for example. Accordingly, employers can study the Xuan Kong Life Stars when making work place decisions whilst employees can use the system to help them go about working productively with their colleagues and superiors, even when disagreements arise.

If you become aware of your own harmful tendencies then you can learn to minimize them so you can advance. Similar benefits can be seen in romantic relationships and friendships. Learning that a Star

7 individual needs their space and independence might help you accommodate this in your dealings with them when you might otherwise have been tempted to be clingy and dependant.

When we understand more about ourselves we can stop ourselves from making mistakes and perhaps forgive certain behaviour in others once we understand where it comes from.

Compatibility Guide

Certain people are, of course, more compatible with each other than others. In partnerships or relationships this takes on a new level of importance. Different Life Stars bestow the qualities of different elements on different people; for example, a Star 1 person has the qualities of water whilst a Star 7 person has the qualities of the Yin Metal element. Just as the elements control, pacify and weaken one another, individuals of the different Stars may dominate, clash with or enrich one another. This book includes a write up of how compatible different Stars are with one another. You may find that a relationship as a Star 1 person with a Star 5 person simply isn't worth the effort. A compatibility guide on each interaction gives you tips on how to best deal with the other Stars for mutual benefit, even taking into account your differences.

Compatible With BaZi Profiling Systems

If you are familiar with the **BaZi Profiling System** then you will be aware that, at first glance, it seems to deal with very similar issues. It can tell us about other preferences and internal view of the world. Do we have an optimistic view of things? Do we blame ourselves too much?

While there is some overlap between the jurisdiction of the Xuan Kong Life Star system and BaZi Profiling System, they are two different systems. They both deal with individual people and their personalities but they are not mutually exclusive. In fact, when studied together, they can be thought of as two pieces of the same puzzle.

The BaZi Profiling System tells us about ourselves and about others. It even tells us things that cannot be observed about others (things people do not communicate). What it can't tell us is how the outside environment plays into the picture. The Xuan Kong Nine Stars help determine *which* qualities are brought out and by what features and external forms in the environment.

Once we know what directions are conducive to good Qi, how external forms (pylons etc) can compound problems related to sectors in the home, which areas of our environment increase the risk of which ailments or even which people can create problems in our lives (compatibility guide) then we can begin shaping our external environment to whatever degree necessary in order to enjoy the most happiness, wealth and success. Xuan

Kong Feng Shui tells you precisely what effect the environment and compass directions will have on which people.

If you are simply interested in learning what makes a person tick rather than making decisions about an ideal environment for them to thrive in then I recommend you take up further study of the BaZi Profiling System. The goal of BaZi is to pinpoint personal deficiencies so that they may be overcome or to highlight personal strengths so that they may be capitalised on.

If you are trying to configure your environment in order to maximize the benefits that your home or place of work bestow upon you in terms of health, wealth and relationships, then the Feng Shui Xuan Kong Life Star system is the one for you.

When you combine the two systems and employ them on yourself you will be able to make the most of your best qualities and then seek out an environment which lets you shine and gives the least resistance. A powerful combination of self improvement and informed decision making!

An Easier Life

Life doesn't have to be difficult. It is possible to effectively dodge conflict, problem situations and health problems if you know they are coming. The Life Stars hold the key to many of the "surprises" that life has in store for us and we can learn to shape our environment to our own advantage. This is exciting stuff! Seeking out the best romantic relationships and business opportunities is a top priority for most people and the power of your Life Star can be called upon in these pursuits.

Even though much is made of the layout of the home with relation to Feng Shui, you won't need to bend over backwards to accommodate the advice given in this book. For instance, where you cannot choose the ideal living floor specified, second and third choices are mentioned. You can take as much or as little from this book as you need without fear of it making you paranoid and prey to "paralysis by analysis". Looking back on your own life, you can most probably think of two or three big mistakes – a bad business deal or choice in romantic partner, perhaps. Avoiding pitfalls of this magnitude in the future is made a whole lot easier when you have some idea of how likely they are to occur. If you can make changes to your environment to further reduce this likelihood then all the better!

I hope that this book expands your world view. Once you know how to utilize them, the Nine Stars can be the harbinger of great fortune instead of misery for you. If you can stay on the 'correct side' of your Star and always position yourself to bask in its positive influence then many happy successes await you.

Joey Yap
July, 2011

 www.facebook.com/joeyyapFB

Author's personal website :
www.joeyyap.com

Academy websites :
www.masteryacademy.com | www.maelearning.com | www.baziprofiling.com

四綠木星命

Four Green Life Star

Life Star 4	Born in
Male	1924, 1933, 1942, 1951, 1960 1969, 1978, 1987, 1996, 2005
Female	1926, 1935, 1944, 1953, 1962 1971, 1980, 1989, 1998, 2007

- Please note that the date for the Chinese Solar Year starts on Feb 4. This means that if you were born in Feb 2 of 2002, you belong to the previous year 2001.

Your Xuan Kong Life Star

Your Xuan Kong Life Star is Gua #4, and your trigram is called Xun. It looks like this:

For the rest of this book, we will refer to your Gua #4 as Life Star 4.

Basic Attributes of Star 4

Your Life Star 4 is of the Yin Wood element, and as such it shares some of the traits of Wood when it manifests its Yin qualities. As the Yin Wood is represented by 'softer' Wood - flowers, reeds, and creepers for example - your attributes are similarly of a softer (but not weaker, as creeping ivy is pretty strong!) and more subtle nature. You are the most romantic of all the Life Stars, and you are imbued with the qualities of grace and beauty.

You are known for you intelligence and creativity. Your Star is strongly associated with scholarly pursuits and the literary arts. As a Star 4 person, you tend to be attuned to your own thoughts and with your senses. The result is that you place a lot on literature, learning, arts, and aesthetics. You are also resourceful and quick-witted. In general, you have a quiet yet self assured personality.

However, like ivy that needs to creep around a tree trunk, you will find that at your less-than-best you can be dependent and clingy an others. This is when you start expecting others to do things for you. Although your charm and wit and conversational ability makes you attractive to others, you can be vague and evasive and keep people at a distance because you're uncertain of how you feel.

Basic Emotions & Temperament

Plus : Kind, gentle, sociable, confident, controlled

Minus: Impulsive, stubborn, calculative, moody, manipulative

方向

YOUR FENG SHUI ESSENTIALS

The Feng Shui Essentials comprise Feng Shui Directions, the effects of the Xuan Kong Nine Stars in various sectors and areas of your home and workspace, and the Five Elements.

Each of these factors interact with your Life Star in different ways that will affect how your Life Star manifests itself and determine whether or not it brings out good or bad qualities in you.

Directions

Directions

Direction is an integral component of understanding Xuan Kong Nine Life Stars. Different directions in your home and your place of work can either accentuate or depreciate the strength of your Life Star.

Favorable Direction will highlight or enhance the positive traits of your Life Star, while an Unfavorable Direction will diminish or weaken your Life Star and bring out some of its negative attributes.

The Life Star numbers are categorized into two groups: the East Group and the West Group. The names 'East Group' and 'West Group' are just to demarcate the Greater and Lesser Yin transformation of the Tai Ji. They do not literally represent directions.

East Group Life Stars include 1, 3, 4 and 9. Those who are Life Stars 2, 6, 7 and 8 belong to the West Group. The following table will give you a quick reference of the Auspicious and Inauspicious compass directions of the East and West Group.

East Group 東命

卦 Gua	生氣 Shen Qi Life Generating	天醫 Tian Yi Heavenly Doctor	延年 Yan Nian Longevity	伏位 Fu Wei Stability	禍害 Huo Hai Mishaps	五鬼 Wu Gui Five Ghosts	六煞 Liu Sha Six Killings	絕命 Jue Ming Life Threatening
坎 Kan 1 Water	東南 South East	東 East	南 South	北 North	西 West	東北 North East	西北 North West	西南 South West
震 Zhen 3 Wood	南 South	北 North	東南 South East	東 East	西南 South West	西北 North West	東北 North East	西 West
巽 Xun 4 Wood	北 North	南 South	東 East	東南 South East	西北 North West	西南 South West	西 West	東北 North East
離 Li 9 Fire	東 East	東南 South East	北 North	南 South	東北 North East	西 West	西南 South West	西北 North West

West Group 西命

卦 Gua	生氣 Shen Qi Life Generating	天醫 Tian Yi Heavenly Doctor	延年 Yan Nian Longevity	伏位 Fu Wei Stability	禍害 Huo Hai Mishaps	五鬼 Wu Gui Five Ghosts	六煞 Liu Sha Six Killings	絕命 Jue Ming Life Threatening
坤 Kun 2 Earth	東北 North East	西 West	西北 North West	西南 South West	東 East	東南 South East	南 South	北 North
乾 Qian 6 Metal	西 West	東北 North East	西南 South West	西北 North West	東南 South East	東 East	北 North	南 South
兌 Dui 7 Metal	西北 North West	西南 South West	東北 North East	西 West	北 North	南 South	東南 South East	東 East
艮 Gen 8 Earth	西南 South West	西北 North West	西 West	東北 North East	南 South	北 North	東 East	東南 South East

The concepts of Favorable and Unfavorable are derived from the Eight Wandering Stars system of the Ba Zhai Eight Mansion Feng Shui 八宅風水.

Each of the 8 directions is governed by a Star. These Wandering Stars will affect each Xuan Kong Life Star in different ways. Each Life Star has four Favorable Directions governed by Auspicious Stars: Sheng Qi 生氣 (Life Generating), Tian Yi 天醫 (Heavenly Doctor), Yan Nian 延年 (Longevity), and Fu Wei 伏位 (Stability).

The four Unfavorable Directions are governed by Inauspicious Stars and include Huo Hai 禍害 (Mishaps), Wu Gui 五鬼 (Five Ghost), Liu Sha 六煞 (Six Killings) and Jue Ming 絕命 (Life Diminishing).

The following diagram shows you the Favorable and Unfavorable Directions for Star 4.

Taking the Direction using a Compass

You will need a compass – or alternatively, the Joey Yap iLuoPan app for iPhone available at the Apple App Store – to determine the direction of your Main Door, Bed and Stove. Hold your compass or iLuoPan at waist level as shown on the illustration below. Your compass or iLuoPan will align to the magnetic North on its own. All you need to know is how to take your direction as indicated on the following pages.

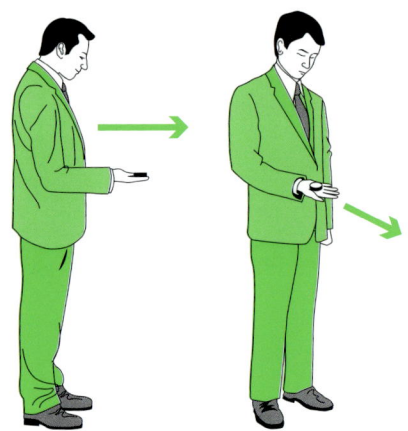

Facing Direction of the Main Door

1. Stand about one foot outside the door looking outwards.

2. Use the square base of your compass to help you align yourself parallel to the door.

3. Read the facing direction on your compass.

Facing Direction of the Bed

1. Measure from the head of the bed where your head is placed when you lie down (the direction the headboard faces) and not the direction your feet face.

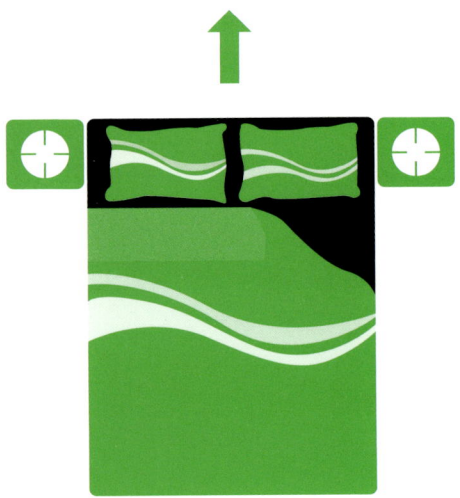

Facing Direction of the Stove

1. For modern (gas or electric) stoves, look at the where direction of the cooking knobs (fire igniters) are pointing to determine its facing direction.

2. For traditional stoves that require wood and fire to work, look for their 'fire mouth' as the facing direction.

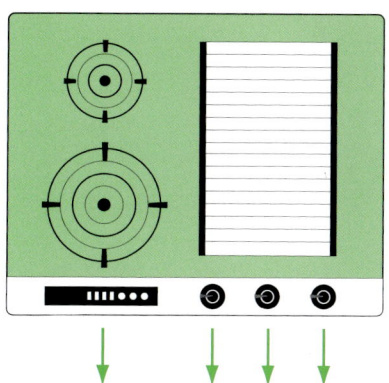

Xuan Kong Nine Life Star

Favorable Directions

North
北 (352.6°-7.5°)

Life Generating
生氣 *(Sheng Qi)*

The basic characteristics of the Sheng Qi Star:

It brings about promotions, career advancements, strong money and wealth luck, potential political power and authority, and all-round success.

The Sheng Qi Star represents life-generating Qi or energy. It also represents the Wood Element, and hence, governs the facets of success, authority, nobility, status and wealth in life. Wood relates to growth and advancement in life, and as such is an extremely auspicious Star to tap into. For you, the North direction taps into the Sheng Qi potential.

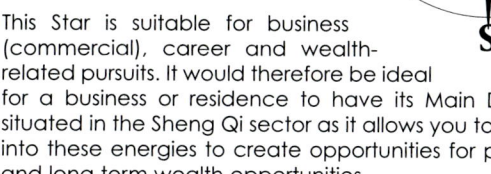

This Star is suitable for business (commercial), career and wealth-related pursuits. It would therefore be ideal for a business or residence to have its Main Door situated in the Sheng Qi sector as it allows you to tap into these energies to create opportunities for profit and long term wealth opportunities.

Sheng Qi is an active star by nature and thus, it is not conducive for rest or sleep-related activities. It is best to avoid having the bed or bedroom located in this sector or for anyone to sleep facing this direction. Use this sector for your work or for active pursuits instead of relaxing ones.

If this sector is missing from a house or is lacking in the office or the premises of a business, the wealth-related aspects of your career or venture will be considerably weakened and it will be a difficult struggle to amass wealth and prosperity.

South
南 (172.6°-187.5°)

Heavenly Doctor
天醫 *(Tian Yi)*

The basic characteristics of the Tian Yi Star:

It brings about general good luck and well-being, as well as positive mentor luck or the presence of sound advisors and guidance.

This Star represents the Earth Element and is therefore the determinant of noble people (mentors) and people of caliber and status. It also denotes your health prospects and physical wellbeing. As such, the Tian Yi Star is best utilized to help generate guidance for your career or for any project which you've embarked upon. It will bring about the help and assistance of others.

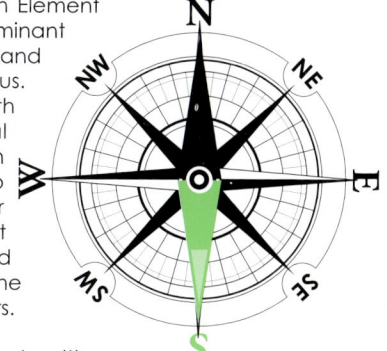

It is also a useful Star for health purposes, and its benefits can be employed when you need to recuperate, recover, or heal from an illness, surgical procedure or health issue.

When the Tian Yin sector is missing from a home or office, your health is likely to suffer because of it. In addition, you will also find help from noble people hard to come by, especially in times of need in life and career matters. You will come across more obstacles and obstructions which you must overcome on your own without the external help of others.

Since the Tian Yi Star represents nobility, it also governs your reputation, respectability, and your oratory powers. It thus has influence on your powers of speech and persuasion, and has some bearing on how you are perceived by others and how well they respond to your verbal overtures.

East
東 (82.6°-97.5°)

Longevity
延年 *(Yan Nian)*

The basic characteristics of the Yan Nian Star:

It prolongs and enhances life and improves the quality of your life. It promotes good communication with others which in turn makes for good relationships.

The Yan Nian Star represents the Metal Element, and as such governs speech and the effectiveness of your words. If you are looking to establish good relationships and rapport with others, you will need the help of this Star, since it governs aspects of successful networking, communication and relationship building.

The Yan Nian Star is important for family harmony and domestic bliss. It is also necessary if you wish to build good relationships with co-workers and colleagues. Essentially, it paves the way for smooth interpersonal relations, seldom plagued by misunderstanding, arguments and flare-ups. As such, the presence of the Yan Nian Star is useful for maintaining harmony.

If you are employed in public relations or marketing and you must interact with clients and customers as part of your daily routine, you will find the Qi brought about by this Star very useful to your career.

Do note that if the Yan Nian sector is missing, harmony and unity will be adversely affected, and relations are likely to be tense or strained. At the very least, you can expect more argument and discord with others.

Southeast
東南 (127.6°-142.5°)

Stability
伏位 (Fu Wei)

The basic characteristics of the Fu Wei Star:

It is a Star that promotes calm and keeps you grounded. It allows for peace of mind and rationality. It also promotes good luck.

The Fu Wei Star represents the Wood Element. When qualities or virtues such as calmness and tranquility are required, this is the Star you need! It promotes peace of mind and heightens clarity of thought, so this is also the Star to use if you need to focus, study or make important decisions.

If you wish to practice mediation or undertake religious and spiritual observances, the Fu Wei Star will provide the energies needed for calm and serenity, enhancing mental health and wellbeing.

- This Star is most suitably applied to libraries, study areas/zones or other places where concentration is necessary. When considering the home or workplace, this Star can help create areas where the mind can be easily quietened and people can reflect and turn inward.

- When the Fu Wei sector is missing from a place, peace of mind will be difficult to attain.

Unfavorable Directions

Northwest
西北 (307.6°-322.5°)

Mishaps
祸害 (Huo Hai)

The basic characteristics of the Huo Hai Star: It denotes potential calamities, accidents, and mishaps. It undermines good efforts and brings about the risk of mistakes and errors.

The Huo Hai Star represents the Earth Element and is the harbinger of mishaps, loss of wealth, sudden (unfortunate) changes or hassles as well as work-related obstacles. What it does is undermine your efforts and bring about sudden obstructions or problems that will result in a loss of time and energy.

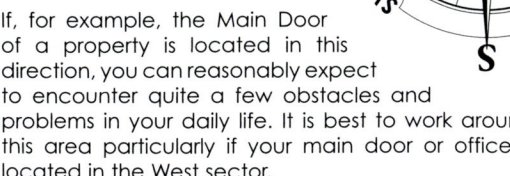

If, for example, the Main Door of a property is located in this direction, you can reasonably expect to encounter quite a few obstacles and problems in your daily life. It is best to work around this area particularly if your main door or office is located in the West sector.

The detrimental effects of a negative star are compounded when it is located within an area that is already affected by negative Feng Shui, so pay attention to the negative structures outside this area.

Southwest
西南 (217.6°-232.5°)

Five Ghosts
五鬼 (Wu Gui)

The basic characteristics of the Wu Gui Star:

It brings about betrayal and treachery through back-stabbing, gossip, and rumors. It also denotes endless bickering and fraught tension brought about by arguments.

The Wu Gui Star represents the Fire Element and is the bringer of betrayal, ill-intentioned gossip, rumours, backstabbing, cruelty, petty people and even subterfuge and sabotage. It generally denotes a sense of unease brought upon by less-than-honest speech.

The presence of Wu Gui in a house causes disloyalty and discord amongst family members, affecting relationships and marriages. If it is present in your work place, then you should also watch out for fights and arguments between your colleagues or subordinates and friction or tension with your superiors.

Negative external forms such as (sharp) pylons and jagged rooftops pointing towards a house further aggravate the effects of this Star.

West
西 (262.6°-277.5°)

Six Killings
六煞 (Liu Sha)

The basic characteristics of the Liu Sha Star:

This Star brings about injuries and accidents. It also denotes the possibility of betrayals and dishonesty, and the risk of potential scandals.

The Liu Sha Star relates to the element of Water and is the harbinger of lawsuits and potential scandals. Legal problems at the workplace or adulterous affairs in relation to your marriage or personal relationships could be brought to light.

This Star is also the harbinger of bodily injury, harm and conditions requiring people to undergo physical surgery. Robberies and theft are also likely, and you will have to be careful about what information you share with others and with the general safety of your personal documents and possessions.

Be mindful of the presence of negative external forms, which will compound the adverse effects of this Star. For instance, a Y-shaped road at the Liu Sha sector will result in scandalous affairs, while negative structures as mentioned earlier will compound and exacerbate the harmful effects of the Liu Sha Star.

Northeast
東北 (37.6°-52.5°)

Life Threatening
絕命 (Jue Ming)

The basic characteristics of the Jue Ming Star:

It brings about the risk of accidents and major illness, and the threat of miscarriage for pregnant women. It also signals potential for great calamity.

This Star represents the Metal Element and it signifies accidents and illnesses. The energies of the Jue Ming Star are quite severe and so are its adverse effects, bringing with it considerable risk.

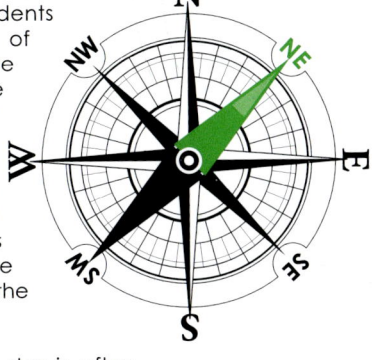

In severe cases, the Jue Ming Star can even cause fatal accidents, ailments or injuries when there are negative external forms outside of the Northeast sector.

It is to no surprise that this star is often regarded as the primary star of misfortune and calamity in the study of Ba Zhai Feng Shui. Other than catastrophes and accidents, it can also cause major loss of wealth and theft as well as the cause of breakups or separation in relationships.

Bed Alignment Direction

One of the key Feng Shui factors of the bedroom is how your bed is placed. For starters, your bed should preferably be pushed against a wall, with the headboard also against it. The most important thing you can do when laying out your bedroom with regards to Feng Shui is to make sure your headboard is aligned with your Favorable Direction.

Facing Direction, in the case of bed alignment, refers to the direction of your headboard. This means it is the direction your head faces when you lie down on the bed, and **not** the direction that your feet face.

As a Star 4, your Bed Alignment Directions are:

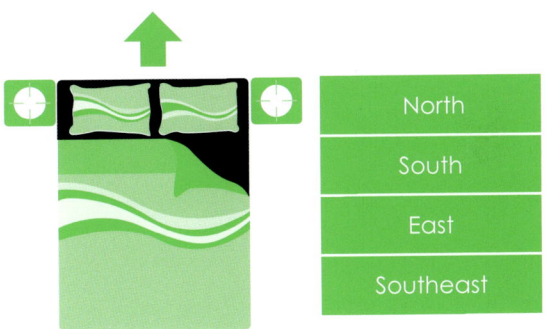

- North
- South
- East
- Southeast

Best Floor

A reality of modern life is that most of us do not live in houses these days, instead living in multi story apartments and condominium blocks.

Some of us are pretty mobile and live a nomad-like lifestyle that may require us to stay in high-rise buildings for certain periods of time. As such, it becomes important to select the right floor to reside in. The objective of this is to achieve elemental affinity between you (the occupant) with the energies of a particular floor.

As you are a Star 4 person of the Wood element, the chart below gives you the best floors for you to live on in terms of first choice, second choice, and third choice.

First Choice	Second Choice	Third Choice
3rd Floor	1st Floor	2nd Floor
8th Floor	6th Floor	7th Floor
13th Floor	11th Floor	12th Floor
18th Floor	16th Floor	17th Floor
23th Floor	21th Floor	22th Floor
28th Floor	26th Floor	27th Floor
33th Floor	31th Floor	32th Floor
38th Floor	36th Floor	37th Floor
43st Floor	41st Floor	42th Floor
48th Floor	46th Floor	47th Floor

Select :
Water shaped buildings & Wood shaped buildings

Avoid :
Metal shaped buildings & Fire shaped buildings

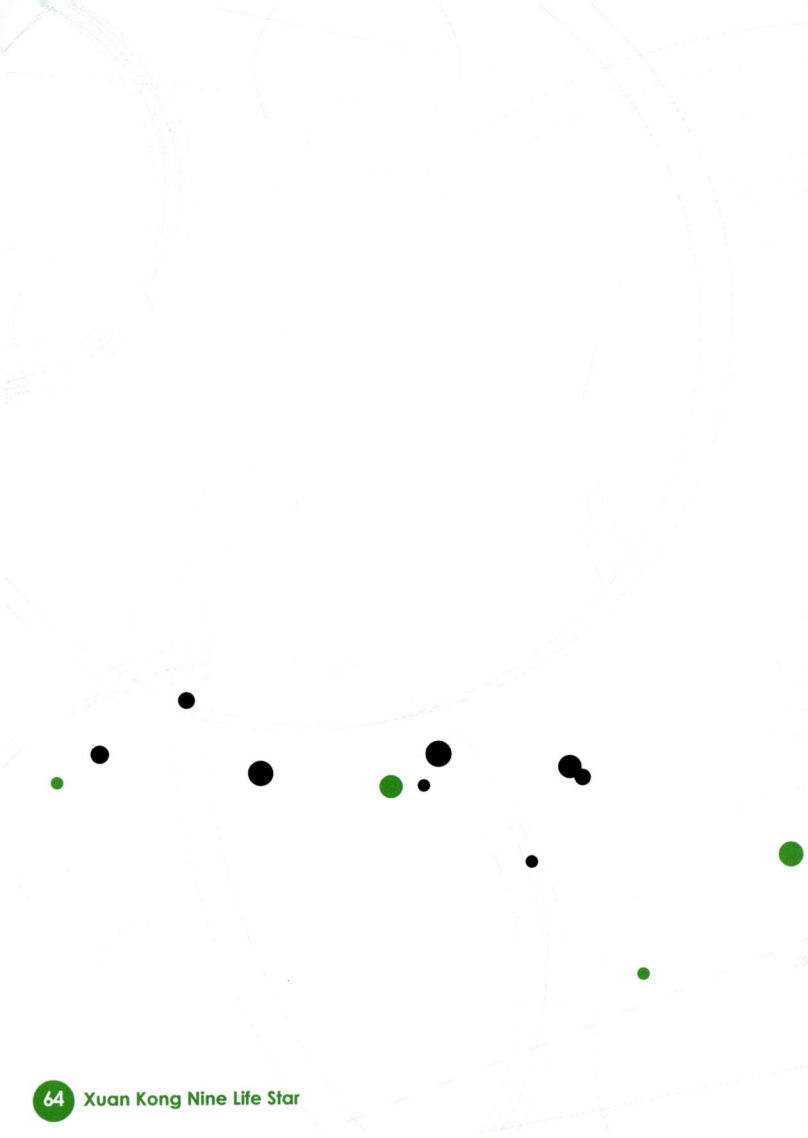

Personal Grand Duke Directions

Identifying the Grand Duke Sector is important. Your Personal Grand Duke Sector relates to your birth year. For example, if you are born in the year of the Rat then the Rat is your Personal Grand Duke and we know that the Rat sector is North 2 .

We want to avoid the harmful properties of this area and as you are a Star 4 person, you can locate your Personal Grand Duke Sector in the following directions:

Personal Grand Duke Directions for Male

MALE Birth Year	Personal Grand Duke	Direction
1915, 1951, 1987, 2023	卯 Mao Rabbit	東 2 East 2
1924, 1960, 1996, 2032	子 Zi Rat	北 2 North 2
1933, 1969, 2005, 2041	酉 You Rooster	西 2 West 2
1942, 1978, 2014, 2050	午 Wu Horse	南 2 South 2

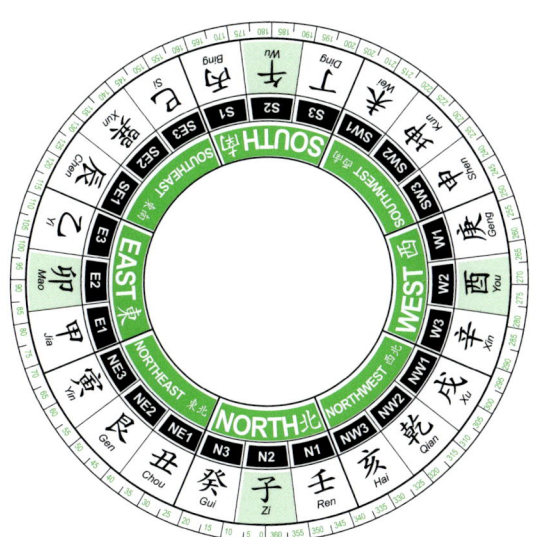

Personal Grand Duke Directions for Female

FEMALE Birth Year	Personal Grand Duke	Direction
1917, 1953, 1989, 2025	巳 *Si* Snake	東南 3 **Southeast 3**
1926, 1962, 1998, 2034	寅 *Yin* Tiger	東北 3 **Northeast 3**
1935, 1971, 2007, 2043	亥 *Hai* Pig	西北 3 **Northwest 3**
1944, 1980, 2016, 2052	申 *Shen* Monkey	西南 3 **Southwest 3**

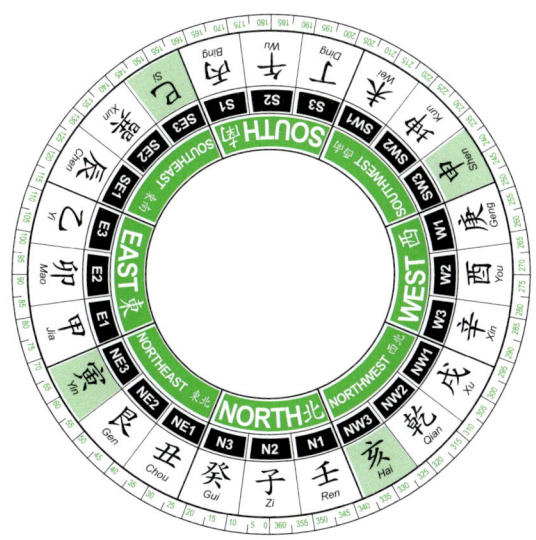

Ideally, you should not have a bathroom or toilet located in these areas of your home above and Sha Qi external features such as pylons, T-junctions, Dead Tree should be avoided. The Sha Qi in the Personal Grand Duke Sector is extremely strong and so all efforts to avoid spending a lot of time in it should be made. It goes without saying that the Personal Grand Duke Sector of your home is not the ideal spot for a bedroom! The Sha Qi in this area of the home is so strong in fact that it is difficult for any further negative Qi to enter!

Personal Clash Directions

Your home will contain Personal Clash Sectors. Spending time in these areas of your home will bring up problems in your life with significant others. As a Star 1 person, you will find your Personal Clash Sectors in the following directions:

Personal Clash Directions for Male

MALE Birth Year	Personal Clash Sector	Direction
1915, 1951, 1987, 2023	酉 You Rooster	西2 **West 2**
1924, 1960, 1996, 2032	午 Wu Horse	南2 **South 2**
1933, 1969, 2005, 2041	卯 Mao Rabbit	東2 **East 2**
1942, 1978, 2014, 2050	子 Zi Rat	北2 **North 2**

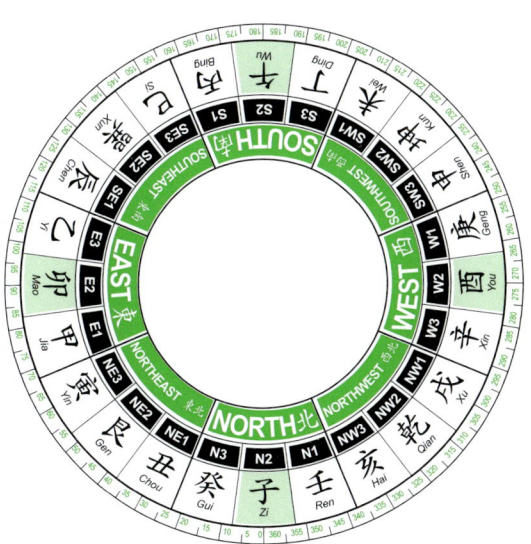

Personal Clash Directions for Female

FEMALE Birth Year	Personal Grand Duke	Direction
1917, 1953, 1989, 2025	亥 Hai Pig	西北 3 Northwest 3
1926, 1962, 1998, 2034	申 Shen Monkey	西南 3 Southwest 3
1935, 1971, 2007, 2043	巳 Si Snake	東南 3 Southeast 3
1944, 1980, 2016, 2052	寅 Yin Tiger	東北 3 Northeast 3

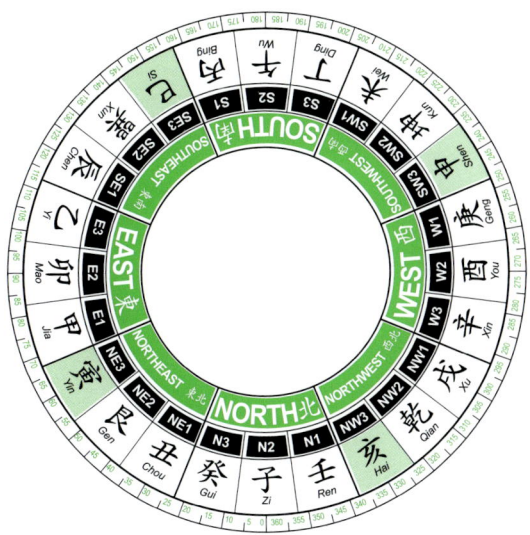

The locations above are a bad place for important features of your home such as the main door, bedroom and kitchen. You should seek to avoid these sectors in the same way you avoid your Personal Grand Duke Sector.

Flying Stars Effects

Each year, the Xuan Kong Flying Stars fly into a different section of a property, be it your residence or your work space. The effects that these Nine Stars have on you will be different depending on your Life Star. In this section you can find out how different Flying Stars in different sectors will effect you with regards to Feng Shui.

The Flying Stars have both negative and positive attributes, but which facets will show when you see a particular Star, depends on the timeliness and the period.

A few of the Nine Stars are inherently negative, a few are inherently positive in nature and some can be both good and bad. Even then, we must remember that the Stars have the capacity to manifest either their positive or negative facets because in Feng Shui, nothing is ever inherently bad or good forever.

When it comes to Flying Stars, it is important to remember this key principle: Forms activate the Stars and the Stars in turn influence the People. This is what you should keep in mind as you read about the effects of the Nine Stars on your Life Star.

1★ → 4 Green Life

The effects of the visiting **#1 White Star** on a **4 Green Life**:

In terms of Feng Shui effects, the presence of the #1 White Star bodes very well for your literary and / or scholarly and academic pursuits. This star will provide you with the energy needed for focus and concentration, particularly if the work you're doing involves research or writing. The sector where #1 White is present will be ideal for you to pursue meditation or religious or spiritual activities in. If you are single, #1 White can bring with it new opportunities in your love life, but this is also true if you're married! Steer clear of flirtation and romantic dalliances that you could come to regret.

2★ → 4 Green Life

The effects of the visiting **#2 Black Star** on a **4 Green Life**:

In terms of Feng Shui effects, the presence of the #2 Black results in conflict between women living in the same area or domestic space. This is particularly true if you're a mother-in-law or a daughter-in-law living with your respective daughter-in-law or mother-in-law. This combination is also bad for elderly ladies of Star 4, as it could bring about some health problems and mental depression. If their bedroom falls under the influence of #2 Black it might be best to use another room for the time being.

3 ★ → 4 Green Life

The effects of the visiting #3 Jade Star on a 4 Green Life:

In terms of Feng Shui effects, the presence of the #3 Jade can be either a boon or a bane to men of the Star 4. This is because you will find that your Peach Blossom luck simply goes through the roof, and you may be surrounded with more romantic attention than you can handle! Beware, though, as not all the people who wish to become involved with you at this time really have your best interests at heart.

Star 4 women likely to be exposed to the effects of #3 Jade need to be careful, however, as it could induce mental volatility and emotional turbulence. Also, you will have to be on the lookout for people entering your life insidious or deceptive intentions.

4★ → 4 Green Life

The effects of the visiting **#4 Green Star** on a **4 Green Life:**

In terms of Feng Shui effects, the presence of the #4 Green is likely to bring about quite a bit of travel for you. Work-related travel may be necessary or holidays may come your way; either way you can expect to move around quite a bit. It also increases your chances of romance, so those of you who are single should make the most of the #4 Green's energies. The Star will also prove beneficial for those of you who are working on academic or scholarly projects, especially if you're working on research or studying for an examination. Bear in mind, however, that the Star can exasperate existing asthma or bronchial illnesses.

5 ★ → 4 Green Life

The effects of the visiting #5 Yellow Star on a 4 Green Life:

In terms of Feng Shui effects, the presence of the #5 Yellow is dangerous for you. The risk of serious diseases and illnesses is hugely increased and breast cancer and infectious disease are made more likely with its presence. Negative effects can also be felt with regards to your finances and gambling losses may afflict you. Keep your guard up and be cautious with your investment choices and when embarking upon new financial ventures.

6 ★ → 4 Green Life

The effects of the visiting **#6 White Star** on a **4 Green Life**:

In terms of Feng Shui effects, the presence of the #6 White brings about some adverse effects for you. If you are married or in a relationship #6 White can be especially problematic as it will mean your interactions are plagued with small problems that escalate, possibly leading to separation or divorce. Health wise, mouth or eye problems may arise. When a negative external form is present, too, depression may affect Star 4 people. Be on the lookout for the onset of these issues.

7★ → 4 Green Life

The effects of the visiting **#7 Red Star** on a **4 Green Life:**

In terms of Feng Shui effects, the presence of the #7 Red is likely to be quite excellent for you, especially in terms of love and romance! New romantic interests may begin to blossom. If you're in a relationship or married, then you can look forward to a smooth path ahead. However, if there are negative structures outside the sector of the #7 Red, then this can bring about family disharmony and plenty of arguments. This is particularly true for the women of the family, and sisters will find themselves at loggerheads more often than usual.

8 ★ → 4 Green Life

The effects of the visiting **#8 White Star** on a **4 Green Life**:

In terms of Feng Shui effects, the presence of the #8 White is likely to bring with it good wealth generating investment opportunities, especially where real estate is concerned. Go the extra mile to maximize benefits. You will need to put in some effort to harness the energies of #8 White but its influence helps ensure success.

If there are negative external structures, however, elderly Star 4 people in particular could suffer from rheumatism.

9★ → 4 Green Life

The effects of the visiting **#9 Purple Star** on a **4 Green Life:**

In terms of Feng Shui effects, the presence of the #9 Purple brings about the likelihood that you will impress others with your intelligence and smarts. More than usual, other people will be attracted to you and find you very appealing, and as such your popularity is bound to rise. Enjoy this for what it is, and reach out to get to know more people and make new friends. It goes without saying that this will bode particularly well for you if you're single!

五行

THE FIVE ELEMENTS

The Five Elements

The element of your Life Star 4 is (Yin) Wood, and it is important that you understand the implications of this. In the study of Chinese Metaphysics and Feng Shui, a basic understanding of the Five Elements is integral to success. This section will briefly outline the role of the Five Elements.

The Five Elements are symbolic representations of energy, or Qi. In Feng Shui and in BaZi, the Five Elements are Earth, Metal, Water, Wood, and Fire. Wood represents benevolence and growth. Yin Wood in particular is of twisting vines and rambling ivy or pretty flowering plants, and denotes elegance and charm, and a resourceful way of getting around things.

In order to understand the elements, it's important to understand their relationship to one another. Each element does not exist in isolation. As such, these elements share three important relationships known as 'cycles' that are fundamental to the understanding of Feng Shui: the Productive Cycle, the Controlling Cycle, and the Weakening Cycle.

Productive Cycle

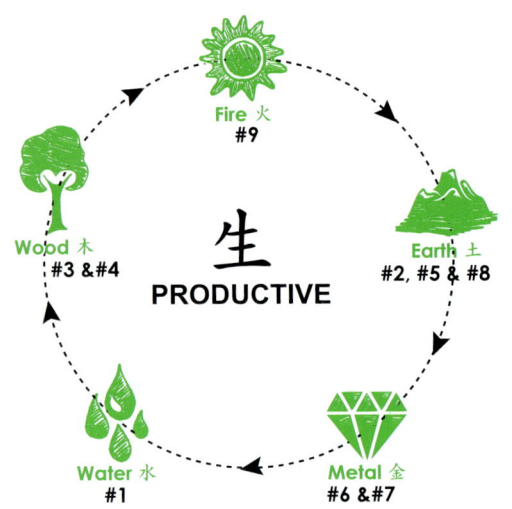

In this cycle,

Water produces Wood
Wood produces Fire
Fire produces Earth
Earth produces Metal
Metal produces Water

This is a cycle where the elements "produce" one another in terms of providing or helping the growth of another. In the case of Water, then, it produces nourishment for trees and plants (i.e. Wood). An element that produces another element means that it strengthens and grows the element that it produces. Here are some simple metaphors might help you visualize this better:

Water waters soil, producing Wood
Wood makes kindling, producing Fire
Fire makes ashes, producing Earth
Earth is mined, producing Metal
Metal melts, producing Water

Controlling Cycle

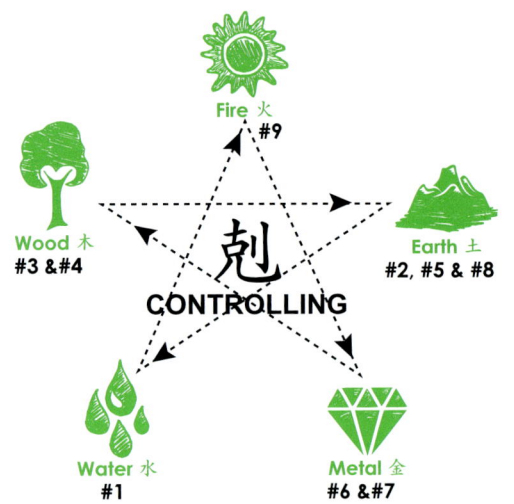

In this cycle,

Fire controls Metal
Metal controls Wood
Wood controls Earth
Earth controls Water
Water controls Fire

This is a cycle where the elements keep each under in "control": an element is countered or subjugated by its controlling element. In this instance, for example, the element of Water controls Fire by putting it out. Here are some simple metaphors to help you visualize it better:

Water extinguishes Fire
Fire melts Metal
Metal cuts Wood
Wood roots tightly grip Earth
Earth contains Water

Weakening Cycle

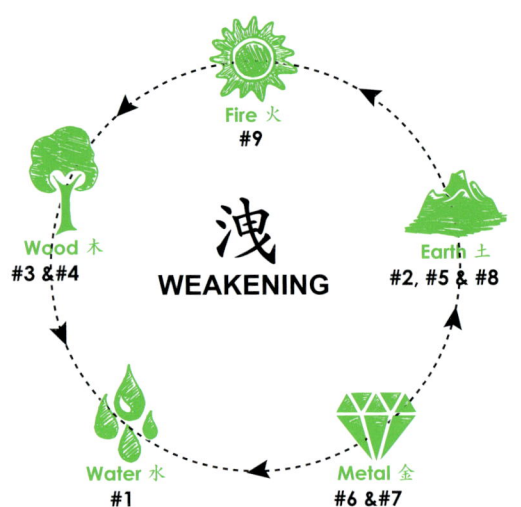

In this cycle,

Water weakens Metal
Metal weakens Earth
Earth weakens Fire
Fire weakens Wood
Wood weakens Water

The Weakening Cycle can be best understood as the reverse of the Productive Cycle, in that the strength of the element is weakened by another in order to keep it in check. Remember, the key to Qi in Feng Shui is balance, and different elements keep other elements from becoming too strong. For example, Wood absorbs Water and therefore weakens it. Again, here are some metaphors for easier visualization:

Water can be partly absorbed by Wood
Wood can be partly burnt by Fire
Fire can be diminished with Earth
Earth is weakened when mined for Metal
Metal is corroded by Water

The following table shows you the Annual Stars for the year 2000 to 2026.

Examine it and figure out where your room lies; in which sector. Take note of the element of that sector and remember that as a Star 4 person, your element is Wood.

2002, 2011, 2020

SE Xun	S Li	SW Kun
6 White METAL	2 Black EARTH	4 Green WOOD
5 Yellow EARTH	7 Red METAL	9 Purple FIRE
1 White WATER	3 Jade WOOD	8 White EARTH
NE Gen	N Kan	NW Qian

(E Zhen on left, W Dui on right)

2003, 2012, 2021

SE Xun	S Li	SW Kun
5 Yellow EARTH	1 White WATER	3 Jade WOOD
4 Green WOOD	6 White METAL	8 White EARTH
9 Purple FIRE	2 Black EARTH	7 Red METAL
NE Gen	N Kan	NW Qian

2004, 2013, 2022

SE Xun	S Li	SW Kun
4 Green WOOD	9 Purple FIRE	2 Black EARTH
3 Jade WOOD	5 Yellow EARTH	7 Red METAL
8 White EARTH	1 White WATER	6 White METAL
NE Gen	N Kan	NW Qian

2005, 2014, 2023

SE Xun	S Li	SW Kun
3 Jade WOOD	8 White EARTH	1 White WATER
2 Black EARTH	4 Green WOOD	6 White METAL
7 Red METAL	9 Purple FIRE	5 Yellow EARTH
NE Gen	N Kan	NW Qian

2006, 2015, 2024

SE Xun	S Li	SW Kun
2 Black EARTH	7 Red METAL	9 Purple FIRE
1 White WATER	3 Jade WOOD	5 Yellow EARTH
6 White METAL	8 White EARTH	4 Green WOOD
NE Gen	N Kan	NW Qian

2007, 2016, 2025

SE Xun	S Li	SW Kun
1 White WATER	6 White METAL	8 White EARTH
9 Purple FIRE	2 Black EARTH	4 Green WOOD
5 Yellow EARTH	7 Red METAL	3 Jade WOOD
NE Gen	N Kan	NW Qian

2008, 2017, 2026

SE Xun	S Li	SW Kun
9 Purple FIRE	5 Yellow EARTH	7 Red METAL
8 White EARTH	1 White WATER	3 Jade WOOD
4 Green WOOD	6 White METAL	2 Black EARTH
NE Gen	N Kan	NW Qian

2000, 2009, 2018

SE Xun	S Li	SW Kun
8 White EARTH	4 Green WOOD	6 White METAL
7 Red METAL	9 Purple FIRE	2 Black EARTH
3 Jade WOOD	5 Yellow EARTH	1 White WATER
NE Gen	N Kan	NW Qian

2001, 2010, 2019

SE Xun	S Li	SW Kun
7 Red METAL	3 Jade WOOD	5 Yellow EARTH
6 White METAL	8 White EARTH	1 White WATER
2 Black EARTH	4 Green WOOD	9 Purple FIRE
NE Gen	N Kan	NW Qian

These Annual Stars shows you the location of the Stars in a property for the duration of the years specified. Based on the year, the Annual Stars will be located in different sectors of the house. Accordingly, different Annual Stars will affect the Feng Shui of your room in different years.

If the Annual Star of your bedroom is of the same element as your Life Star then the outcome is likely to be prosperous (Productive Cycle). If the Annual Star is your Life Star's controlling element (Controlling Cycle), then the result is likely to be stressful – although this combination is still desirable. But if the Annual Star element is the countering element (Countering Cycle) of your Life Star, then the combination is an unfavorable or inauspicious one for you. (Special note: the #5 Yellow Star is generally an undesirable Annual Star for your bedroom regardless of your Life Star.)

Think about the way the element of the Annual Star and your element (Wood) interact.

Besides the Annual Stars of the year, there also other factors to be considered. These include the Flying Stars chart of your specific house or property with the Sitting and Facing Stars. Advanced students may want to read *Xuan Kong Flying Stars Feng Shui* for further information. These Stars also affect the evaluation of the impact of the Xuan Kong Flying Stars on your property. There are many other ways of assessing the Feng Shui of a property, and it's important to understand that all these factors play an important and related role.

Characteristics of Star 4

We all have our "good days" and "bad days". Feng Shui seeks to help isolate why this happens and provide advice that you can use to make every day a "good day" where you are in your element. This section outlines the good and bad characteristics of your Life Star. In a positive sector of your house or work, the positive attributes of your Life Star will be further enhanced, and you will display more of these characteristics. In a negative sector, the positive attributes will be diminished and the negative attributes will begin to show through. Your bad characteristics will take center stage.

The Good

Scholarly

Star 4 is known to imbue the characteristics of a scholar. As a Star 4 person you place value on learning, beauty, and achievement through literary and artistic pursuits. You have a gift for studying and strong critical thinking abilities. You will be happiest when immersed in the world of academia. You like all things creative and you take pleasure simply immersing yourself in deep thinking.

Adaptive

You are quick witted and you can think on your feet. This enables you to come up with ingenious solutions to work around problems. As such, you can adapt to most situations quite well and you are not afraid to change direction at the last minute in order to gain better leverage. At your best you can be flexible and fleet-footed in your approach to life.

Friendly

You are the most romantic of the Life Stars, and this means that you can be quite flirtatious and charming with the people you find attractive. As such, romance tends to follow you wherever you go. Your engaging communication and listening skills that enables you to make friends with ease. You have an affable and easygoing personality that tends to put others at ease, as well.

Liberal

You are open-minded in nature and you do not judge others too quickly. You value refinement in thought, and would rather explore the nuances of an argument or position before denouncing it as good or bad. Star 4 people are likely to be both prudent and compassionate in considering others' viewpoints, and as such are fairly broad-minded in their thinking.

壞

The Bad

Fickle

At an unhealthy level or state, however, Star 4 people can be very fickle-minded and are prone to changing their opinions very quickly. This means that you may have a mercurial reaction to certain issues and thus lack staying power. You may start something but fail to finish it. You can become vague and find yourself listening to other people's opinions instead of formulating your own.

Dependent

You can be quite complacent in accepting that others may have to do things for you. This can be a weakness, as you become too reliant on others in order to get ahead or achieve something. You must stem your dependence on others as much as possible because your own resourcefulness is more than enough. In personal relationships, your dependency means you can sometimes become clingy.

Proud

You have a healthy ego, and this is good, but in an unhealthy state this means that you tend to carry a little too much pride. As the old saying goes, pride comes before a fall. You may feel a sense of superiority over others and this can leave you unwilling to give up 'face' or risk tarnishing your reputation by swallowing your pride. This is one way for you to keep yourself distant from others even while maintaining a facade of friendliness.

Impractical

If you allow your absent-mindedness to get the best of you, then you can become gullible and impractical. You must make sure that you must stay sharp and correctly assess situations. Maintain a realistic appraisal of your own abilities and limitations. Being impractical can also make you greedy in that you want more, but more may not necessarily be always good for you.

職業和財富

CAREER AND WEALTH

Characteristics at Work

As a Star 4 person, you may display some of these basic characteristics in professional situations at the workplace and in relation to your career. Being aware of your own key characteristics will help you understand why you act and react to situations, people, and tasks in the way you do.

This section outlines the good and bad characteristics of your Life Star. In a positive sector of your house or work, the positive attributes of your Life Star will be further enhanced, and you will display more of these characteristics. In a negative sector, the positive attributes will be diminished and the negative attributes will begin to show through. Your bad characteristics will take center stage.

• Communicative

You have charm in spades and at the workplace this is definitely a plus-point in terms of networking and getting ahead. You can be quite silver-tongued and possess the ability to make others feel at ease. The great emphasis you place on elegant speech enables you to take your time with the way you articulate yourself in order to prevent possible misunderstandings. You can also be persuasive, a coveted skill in terms of dealing with clients and customers.

• Smart

It goes without saying that one of the key characteristics of a Star 4 person is a quick and agile mind. You are smart on the job and those you work with value your ability to analyze situations and come up with new approaches to problems and fresh opinions. Indeed, you strive to think outside the box and dislike having to adhere to the status quo.

• Imaginative

One of the perks of having a mind that is flexible and open-minded is that you're capable of seeing stars where others only see the sky! This means you often have a creative approach to solutions and problems and take pride and pleasure in analyzing the situation and implementing a fresh solution. You make an effort to understand a task before proceeding.

• Insightful

You always seek to gain insight when dealing with work tasks as well as about the people you work with. Star 4 people are generally very sensitive and make an effort to empathize with others in order to understand their point of view and know where they're coming from. You are sharp and perceptive and thus tend to score quite high on the emotional intelligence scale.

Suitable Job Roles

• Writer, publishing

Most Star 4 people have a gift with words, and this is because reading is something they tend to typically enjoy. You have a large vocabulary and a unique way of expressing things which gives you a talent for writing and for dealing with words.

This can mean that career as an author, an opinion journalist, a wordsmith in advertising, or in film and TV as a scriptwriter may be right up your street. Furthermore, careers in publishing and the book industry are well-suited to you.

• Scholar, academic, professor

You naturally gravitate towards jobs which require study, thinking skills and the acquisition of further knowledge. As such, a life in academia is one that plays nicely to your strengths. You will also be suitable for a job which allows you teach, for example in a professorship, particularly on subjects that capitalize on your interest in the arts, philosophy, and humanity.

• Arts (performing, broadcasting)

Star 4 personality attributes dovetail perfectly with the requirements of the arts you're well suited to a career as a musician or artist or something to do with talent and creativity. You know where your artistic talents lie and you

will be able to make a rewarding living from them. Some Star 4 personalities also thrive in a life in under the spotlight, whether as a broadcast host or as a stage or film actor.

• Marketing, communications

You are a sociable person which means that over the years you have developed a strong grasp on how other people behave and think. You may be ideally suited to a career where you both communicate with others and cater to their needs. Careers in marketing and public relations rely on communication and unique branding. When you bring your adaptive mind and creative talent to the table, you will be able to craft campaigns and strategies that will be of value to your clients.

Career and Wealth Guide

- ## Focus on decision-making

    You often come up with great ideas or plans but at your weakest you can allow your thoughts to drift or wander. This is likely to happen when you train your attention on too many disparate things, instead of focusing your attention on one thing, thereby making it hard for you to make decisions and execute them. Cultivate a clear sense of focus and you will learn to trust your own decisions.

• Stay attentive to people

You have a way with people, and this should be something you use to your advantage at the workplace! Invite people into your thought-processes and treat them with the compassion and interest that you feel. Don't stem your people-curiosity, as others will be flattered and encouraged by your attention and respond in kind, which will be valuable in terms of forming social networks for the short-term and in the long-run.

• Want less

This is particularly true where your finances are concerned! When in an unhealthy state, you can become particularly insatiable and covetous, and may be tempted to dabble in all things that may potentially bring you more money. However, this can lead you to get involved in risky ventures. Be ambitious and forward-thinking, by all means, but keep your expectations moderate and don't be afraid to turn down opportunities if they are too risky.

• Strive for practicality

Your head tends to be in the clouds, and sometimes your attention wanders and you expect other people to step in with some sound rational advice instead of thinking things through from A-Z on your own. In matters of finance, you cannot afford to live with your head in the clouds! Come up with a clear, legible budget that ensures you never run the risk of acquiring a mounting debt or engaging in foolish financial ventures or investments.

• Do the hard part first

You give up easily when you encounter a problem in a project. You do not have a realistic ability to weigh up how difficult something will be when you embark upon it so when problems arise you are shocked! You can try and ignore difficult parts of a project by working only on the easy parts, getting into trouble when a deadline comes along. Work on the tough parts first instead of leaving them to the last minute.

Famous Personalities :

Michael Bloomberg,
Steve Wynn,
Stephen Hawking,
Irene Rosenfeld

人際關係

RELATIONSHIPS

Guide for Relationships

As a Star 4 person, you are one of the most romantic Stars of all. What this means is that you enjoy the beauty and drama and excitement of a passionate romance. You enjoy cultivating love as thought it were a flowering plant. As such, you tend to be popular and will find that others are easily attracted to you, too. Your sense of passion and interest in many things allows you to connect to a variety of people, and others are drawn in by your intelligent, charming, and sophisticated ways.

You do run the risk of becoming 'lost' in love if you don't put a break on your fantasies, however. You may find it hard to make the hard decisions pertaining to your relationship, and you can fall into the trap of constantly pondering about the small small things and worrying over nothing. This is hardly ideal because it stops you from simply enjoying the other persons company and going along for the ride! If you run into problems or obstacles in your relationship, your dislike for practicality in love may result in you not being able to take the proper stand when it is required.

Because you tend to be a 'yes person' in love, you may also run the risk of being uncertain how to decide in terms of partners. In some extreme cases, you may not know how to turn down someone who's trying to get your attention or love. Star 4 people at an unhealthy level tend to say 'yes' to the wrong person, perhaps getting into less than ideal marriages and ending up with some regrets.

This particular inability to say no will also put you at risk for extramarital affairs or dalliances, and divorce and multiple marriages could be a possibility for a Star 4 person. That is not to say that you're a bad partner – on the contrary, when you're healthy, you can be one of the best: warm, engaged, considerate, and loving. During the good times, your married life and family can be joyful. But this means that you need to be more of a realist and cultivate a more pragmatic perspective in dealing with your own feelings and those of your partner or spouse. Try and form a realistic and practical appraisal of whether or not things are working out and make the right decisions based on this, even if they are difficult.

Star 4 in relationships:

Star 4 people are strongly attracted to love and romance and often meet partners unexpectedly. They sometimes have trouble making decisions and often miss good opportunities.

健康

HEALTH

Guide for Health

Body parts and organs that are related to Star 4: Liver, gallbladder, stomach, spleen.

In times of ill health, your liver, gallbladder, stomach, spleen and pancreas will probably be the organs and body parts which play up. Watch out for potential liver disease as well as the prominence of gallstones. Stomach problems can also arise in the form of constipation, irritable bowel syndrome, gastritis and potential ulcer. Stress and constant worrying on your part during tough times can result in bad eating habits that further contribute to this problem. Keep an eye on your alcohol intake to help guard against liver disease and pay heed to the way different foods affect your digestive habits.

Your immune system can also frequently come under attack, and this means that you're quite susceptible to colds and flu and allergies unless you take the proper precautions to ward off germs. You may find yourself frequently suffering from a sore throats. Mental and physical health are inter-related to one another, and the more you worry or fall prey to stress, the weaker your physical body will become over time. Your lungs can be weak, and you must keep a keen eye on your breathing and endurance so that you will detect changes quickly and seek treatment early if you contract infections.

Weak nerves are a problem for Star 4 types, particularly if you're scared, worried, or anxious. You are susceptible to agitation and anxiety when overworked and the weak nerves this brings on can lead to other health problems, too. As such, it is imperative that you focus on cultivating a healthy lifestyle that does not allow stress to build up so that your body in turn remains strong. Although you

are already energetic and inspired, you may have to make a further commitment to regular exercise and cultivate good habits in life in terms of health, diet, and nutrition, in order to withstand the occasional illness brought about by stress and worry.

Potential health concerns:

Liver-related problems (cirrhosis)

Common cold and influenza

Breathing difficulties

Flatulence & 'wind' in the stomach

Arthritis

Stiff neck, waist and hips

Tennis elbow

COMPATIBILITY WITH OTHER LIFE STARS

This section examines your compatibility as a Star 4 with other people who have the same and different Stars. No person goes through life completely alone.

Relationships with others form the bedrock of good career networking. Friendships and relations with loved ones, spouses, partners and family make everything worth while. It is necessary to understand how compatible people with different Stars are to prevent conflict and missed opportunities. Bear in mind that issues of compatibility are not definite or set in stone. There are exceptions to every rule. In addition, **the quality of Feng Shui** in your environment helps dictate whether positive or negative traits in people manifest themselves and thus it weighs in on the quality of your relationships with those people. This section serves as a good guide on your relationships with other people of different Stars.

At a glance, Star 4 people are often viewed as attractive by most others. They find your charming and personable and they will take pleasure in your company. You will typically enjoy good relations with Stars 3, 1, 2, 5 and 8. Relationships with Stars 4, 6, 7, and 9, however, can alternately prove problematic,

complicated or even dangerous relationships, depending on the specific personality of the people in question.

Because you are a Wood Star, you need to be careful when dealing with Metal stars (who counter your Wood). Don't be careless or negligent in your relationship with Stars 6 and 7. Star 4 people will most probably become enemies in your life as there is a greater chance that your personalities will clash producing conflict than there is that you will bond. Interactions with those of Star 9, a Fire Star, may start out well but will not be beneficial in the long run because Fire weakens Wood.

You have good affinity with the other Stars, but particularly Star 1 people. This is because Star 1 is a Water Star and Water produces Wood. Star 1 folk will turn out to be excellent at providing support and helping you out during times of need. There is a good chance of long-term relationships with Star 1 people.

The chart below lists element people or sectors you can utilize to improve your compatibility with other Star people.

	Compatibility with others Stars (Individuals)	Seek help from this element people or use this sector
Star 4	Stars 2, 5 & 8 (Earth Element)	Fire
	Stars 3 & 4 (wood Element)	Earth
	Stars 6 & 7 (Metal Element)	Water
	Star 9 (Fire Element)	Earth
	Star 1 (Water Element)	Wood

巽 SE Xun	離 S Li	坤 SW Kun
4 Green WOOD	**9** Purple FIRE	**2** Black EARTH
3 Jade WOOD	**5** Yellow EARTH	**7** Red METAL
8 White EARTH	**1** White WATER	**6** White METAL
艮 NE Gen	坎 N Kan	乾 NW Qian

震 E Zhen · 兌 W Dui

The following pages will explain in detail the compatibility factor of a Star 4 person with people of all other nine Stars through the Compatibility Meter. The Compatibility Guides give you tips for managing the relationships in question.

| **4** White | compatibility with | **1** White |

Compatibility Meter

When a Star 4 person comes together with a Star 1 person, the union is likely to be productive. You have a lot in common which makes an initial connection forthcoming: you are both creative and share an appreciation of the arts. In fact, you are actually well suited for the same kind of careers – you might both make good writers or creative types which means that you are quite likely to bump into Star 1 individuals in your workplace! You are gentle and warm when at your best which a Star 1 individual will appreciate and you in turn appreciate the fact that a Star 1 individual listens to you and cares about your needs. Your compatibility has its roots in the fact that Star 1 people are of the Water element, which is very good for the Wood of your Star 4, thus leading to a relationship where you will both

find yourselves enjoying the benefits of growth and strength. Star 1 individuals may have some difficulty reaching you if you become distant with them and become impatient if they feel they cannot connect.

Compatibility Guide

One of the easiest ways to allow this valuable relationship to fail is if you take the help and attention of the Star 1 person for granted. The Star 1 person's help is likely to be offered in a sincere and unselfish manner, so do not betray their trust by taking advantage of it. You often become clingy as time goes on and start expecting others to do things for you. In a relationship this can cause a rift with a Star 1 individual as they are highly independent. For a relationship with them to work you must remember to hold back with your feelings of dependency and retain your own autonomy. This can be difficult for you in romantic relationships because you are prone to overindulging your romantic tendencies!

| **4** White | compatibility with | **2** Black |

Compatibility Meter

When a Star 4 person comes together with a Star 2 person, the result is good, especially for the Star 2 individual. This is because of your ability to 'charm' out the best – the talent, as it were, of Star 2 people, where they might otherwise have a tendency to be inert. As such, you will find yourself in the role of a sort of supporter, nurturer, and mentor – particularly if this is a work-based relationship or a professional partnership. The Star 2 person will find lots of reasons to admire you, and will not hold back in showing this! You are great at coming up with unique ideas and solutions but not so great at implementing them so you may wish to employ the practical mind of a Star 2 individual to help turn your plans into reality. In a relationship you may find yourself leading the way.

Compatibility Guide

The relationship between you and a Star 2 person will be mutually beneficial, but you will need to gain their trust in order for them to help you bring out their hidden qualities! Don't give up and move on if results do not immediately materialize. If you take your role as a mentor too far then the Star 2 individual can build up a dependency for your presence, stifling their own growth and autonomy. This is unhealthy so you must retain a certain distance, especially professionally. If you become involved in a relationship, Star 2 people are unlikely to tell you when you have stepped out of line and they will forgive again and again. Do not take advantage of this and make a concentrated effort not to let the relationship dissolve into one where you walk all over the other person and assume they will always be around, because you will miss them when they do eventually leave.

|  4 White | compatibility with | 3 Jade |

Compatibility Meter

When you and a Star 3 person get together, the outcome is good for friendship and romance. This is because there is a force of mutual attraction that will keep the relationship going. You find their drive and straight manner of dealing with issues attractive. There will be plenty of warmth and sharing as the easy camaraderie keeps the both of you drawn to each other. Trust and understanding built over time will be the glue for this relationship. You are less suited, however, to a business relationship. You may be prone to chop and change and might have difficulty adhering to plans they lay down. This can create friction with a Star 3 person who will expect things to be done by the book! Even if you can think of new ways to achieve things they are unlikely to yield to your suggestions which can frustrate you as you usually think you know best.

Compatibility Guide

Star 3 individuals are intense. They need things done urgently and you are prone to going overboard, especially romantically, before the time is right. When Star 3 people fall for someone, they fall in a big way and put a lot of energy into a relationship, no matter how fledgling. All of this means that there is a risk that you can become deeply involved with one another before either of you are really ready! Therefore, what will be important in this relationship is the refusal to be impulsive. Don't rush into things. The onus might be on you to make sure that things move forward at a measured pace because the Star 3 person naturally possesses quite an aggressive and forceful personality. Aim for moderation, as either one of you can go into extremes. Balance and stability will be important in order to build solid trust and understanding between Star 3 and Star 4.

| **4** White | compatibility with | **4** White |

Compatibility Meter

When you and a Star 4 person get together, things can go either way. Being of the same Star, it is likely that you will share similar creative interests. This can lead to collaboration or inspiration. If you are entering into a professional partnership however you may find that very little gets done as you are both impractical and fickle. Friendships, however can thrive and conflict is unlikely to arise so long as you are both in a positive frame of mind where you are gentle and sociable. You will also probably hit it off romantically with other Star 4 individuals as you are both socially adept, witty and skilled in the art of conversation. Any ensuing relationship will likely be exciting and dramatic and passionate; you both love to be in love! It is only in the long term that some problems can arise.

Compatibility Guide

If entering into a business partnership, make sure that you come up with a realistic plan together... and then execute it! You would do well to bring in a third party of a different Star who can help you keep things on track and bring your expectations back down to earth if need be. Romantically, things are likely to go well in the beginning. In the long term, any disagreement or argument can make you liable to become distant with one another. Attempts to patch things up may not be immediately successful as can you can both be irrational when filled with extreme emotions. It will be important to recognize this trait and make a conscious effort to be rational while making decisions in relation to each other, putting aside your own pride for the common good.

| **4** White | compatibility with | **5** Yellow |

Compatibility Meter

When you and a Star 5 person get together, the results are typically positive. You are a great conversation maker and Star 5 individuals are assertive and strong socially which means that you are unlikely to be bored in each others company. If this is business partnership or working one, both your personalities can offset each other in complementary ways, where your advantages of good communication skills can probably do a good job in making up for any potential shortcomings in collaboration. They are highly organized and focused, unlike you, but you may be able to bring creative ideas and lateral thinking to the table. Together, good headway made in professional interests that serve both you and the Star 5 person. When in a negative frame of mind, you will be drawn intrinsically to Star 5 individuals because

of their authoritative, strong personality. They can serve as your rock. You may find that you need their strength during difficult times and they are loyal and even caring despite their hardened exterior.

Compatibility Guide

Star 5 individuals need to learn to kick back and relax which means that you may need to chip away at first in order to forge a "fun" friendship. In terms of productivity, for your partnership with the Star 5 person to work, you need to pull your own weight. Don't succumb to your tendency to sit back and expect other people to do things for you! There is a strong risk that you will let this happen because Star naturally take charge and lead the way! If you come to expect things to be handed to you on a silver platter, disgruntlement will ensue. Since this is likely to work as a partnership, you will have to be serious, committed, and mature or you are liable to irritate the Star 5 individual quickly with your lack of contribution. This rings true for all kinds of relationship with them.

| **4** White | compatibility with | **6** White |

Compatibility Meter

When you and a Star 6 person get together, the resulting dynamic will be complex. You will probably respect them and the noble stance they take on many issues but you may find that their sense of righteousness makes them inflexible in a world where not everyone else is willing to play by the rules. In a business setting, you may find that together you get very little done! You may both end up standing around with your arms crossed when you should be getting things done as you are impractical and Star 6 people are more suited to delegating than actually working. On a personal level, many Star 6 people are intelligent and talented like you. In this case, there will be plenty of things they can teach and share with you – especially with regards to principles, leading to personal growth. In this sense, they can be your Noble People who will guide you towards bigger and better things. Because there is strong basic affinity and mutual attraction

between Star 4 and Star 6 people, conflict and arguments are likely to be short lived and easily put in the past. Romantic relationships will be fraught with difficult from the get go as Star 6 individuals are famously distant and guarded. This is not conducive to the kind of passionate whirlwind romance you have in mind!

Compatibility Guide

If the Star 6 person is a helpful, nurturing one, you stand to gain a lot from them on a personal level. On the other hand, Star 6 people can become controlling and demanding if you let them. They do not generally possess malignant attitudes and are known to wield power responsibility but nevertheless, you should be aware that your gentle personality might make you a target for dominance in their eyes. Short of cowing to them, you should cut your losses, be strong, and move on if you feel things aren't working out. You are both stubborn and compromise in the situation outlined above is unlikely.

| **4** White | compatibility with | **7** Red |

Compatibility Meter

When you and a Star 7 person come together, your charms will attract the Star 7 person. They know just what to say in every situation to please people and have an innate thirst for life so your initial interactions will be exciting! The Star 7 person will be taken in by the combination of intelligence, and confidence you possess. If this is a friendship or even a relationship, you will find that they might go out of their way to spend time with you and will lavish you with attention, and you're likely to enjoy it! The vivacious nature and taste for extravagance that Star 7 individuals have means that you will see them as good candidates for the kind of dramatic, all consuming romance you enjoy being involved in. Be aware that they do have an arrogant side and a taste for luxury which

you may struggle to keep up with. You might also struggle to connect on anything more than a superficial level, making long term commitment unlikely.

Compatibility Guide

You will need to keep up with appearances in order to make things work. If the Star 7 individual feels you are somehow beneath them or unable to keep up then they may take on a condescending attitude towards you which you may have to struggle against. When you are with the Star 7 person, particularly if we're talking about a friendship or a romantic relationship, you have to be able to curtail your demands for 'more'. Being too demanding will scare off the Star 7 person. Always remember that a Star 7 individuals life revolves around attention – they need it and they thrive when receiving it. Your tendency to be distant will make them look elsewhere if you do not learn to control it.

| **4** White | compatibility with | **8** White |

Compatibility Meter

When you and a Star 8 person come together, the result is likely to be lukewarm but beneficial. In your connection to a Star 8 person, there is unlikely to be chemistry or even much laughter and fun. Star 8 individuals are placid and cool and this does not make for much excitement. Fortunately, from a business or work point of view, they are reliable and versatile. Because of this, you will work best with these people when working towards mutual professional goals. Even when disagreements arise, Star 8 individuals will remain tight lipped. Conflict, therefore, will be kept out of your interactions with this person which is good in a work environment, particularity if you are the superior and you need someone who does things without arguing and questioning you. Romantic involvement will be inadvisable due to your incompatible world views.

Compatibility Guide

In order to make this work, you and the Star 8 person will probably be better off focusing on getting your goals met instead of trying to be friends. As such, this is bound to be a business venture or some form of work partnership. Trying to force each other to be friends outside of the professional sphere may place undue strain even in your working environment, so keep it casual and professional for success. They will not provide the excitement or drama you seek in romance, being slow, cautious and inexpressive.

| **4** White | compatibility with | **9** Purple |

Compatibility Meter

When you and a Star 9 person come together, things will start off with a bang. Sharing an eye for all things creative, both of you will admire and appreciate each others talents and good qualities. In fact, you might even feel like old friends right from the get-go! Both of you will assume that the other is equally-caring. In the long run, however, a Star 9 person could weaken you as they are known to be more controlling and demanding than you. Whether or not they will weaken you depends a lot on how much of your own person you're allowed to be in the relationship. Be wary of your inclination to become dependent and clingy because the other person, perhaps unwittingly, will take advantage of this to your detriment.

Compatibility Guide

In your connection with the Star 9 person, care should be taken – especially if this is a romantic relationship. You need to be your own person, and it could become dangerous if you start 'losing' yourself in the Star 9 person and sacrificing time with your own friends and family or your own interests, pursuits, and ambitions only to accommodate the Star 9 person's demands. If it's not reciprocal, hit the brakes and scale back – the relationship might be best not pursued further.

About Joey Yap

Joey Yap first began learning about Chinese Metaphysics from masters in the field when he was fifteen.

Despite having graduated with a Commerce degree in Accounting, Joey never became an accountant. Instead, he began to give seminars, talks and professional Chinese Metaphysic consultations in Malaysia, Singapore, India, Australia, Canada, England, Germany and the United States, becoming a household name in the field.

By the age of twenty-six, Joey became a self-made millionaire and in 2008, he was listed in The Malaysian Tatler as the Top 300 Most Influential People in Malaysia and Prestige's Top 40 Under 40.

His practical and result-driven take on Feng Shui and BaZi sets him apart from other older, traditional masters and practitioners in the field. He shows people how the ancient teachings can be utilized for tangible REAL world benefits. The success he and his clients enjoy, thanks to his advice, is positive proof that Feng Shui and BaZi Astrology works, whether everyone believes in it or not!

Today, Joey has helped and worked with governments and the wealthiest people in Singapore, Hong Kong, China, Malaysia and Japan. His clients include multinationals, developers, tycoons and royalties. On Bloomberg, he is featured on-air as a regular guest on the subject of Feng Shui annual forecasts. He is retained by twenty-five top Malaysian property developers to help determine suitable candidates to take top management, change their space and Feng Shui mechanism, the way they make decisions, and understand the natural cosmic energies that can influence their decision-making.

Every year he conducts his 'Feng Shui and Astrology' seminar to a crowd of more than 3500 people at the Kuala Lumpur Convention Center. He also takes this annual seminar on a world tour to Frankfurt, San Francisco, New York, Las Vegas, Toronto, Sydney and Singapore.

The Joey Yap Consulting Group is the world's largest and first specialized metaphysics consultation firm. His consultancy, and professional speaking and training engagements with Microsoft, HP, Bloomberg, Citibank, HSBC and many more have seen the benefits of Classical Feng Shui and BaZi find their way into corporate environment and culture. Celebrities, property developers and other large organizations turn to Joey when they need the best.

After years of field-testing and fine-tuning his teachings, he has put together a team in the form of Joey Yap Research International. The objective of this Research Team is to scientifically track and verify the positive impact of Feng Shui and BaZi on subjects and ultimately to assist more people in achieving their life goals.

The Mastery Academy of Chinese Metaphysics which Joey founded teaches thousands of students from all around the world about Classical Feng Shui, Chinese Astrology and Face Reading. Many graduates have gone on to become successful in their own right, becoming sought after consultants, setting up their own consultancy businesses or even becoming educators, passing on Chinese Metaphysics knowledge to others.

Joey has also created the Decision Referential Technology™, offering decision reformation training on how to make better decisions in business and in personal life. He has led his team of highly trained consultants to help clients create more positive change in corporate boardrooms and increase production in their companies, helping people see their business outlook for each year so they may anticipate, plan and execute their strategies successfully.

Joey's work has been featured regularly in various popular global publications and networks like Time, Forbes, the International Herald Tribune and Bloomberg. He has also written columns for The New Straits Times, The Star and The Edge – Malaysia's leading newspapers. He has achieved bestselling author status with over sixty-five books, which have sold more than three million copies to-date.

His success is not limited to matters of Feng Shui and BaZi. Although his success is a product of them, he is also a successful entrepreneur, leading his own companies and property investment portfolio. When not teaching metaphysics or consulting around the world, Joey is a Naruto-fan, avid snowboarder and is crazy for fruits de mer.

Author's personal website :

 www.joeyyap.com

Joey Yap on Facebook:

 www.facebook.com/JoeyYapFB

MASTERY ACADEMY
OF CHINESE METAPHYSICS
Your **Preferred** Choice to the Art & Science of Classical Chinese Metaphysics Studies

Bringing **innovative** techniques and **creative** teaching methods to an ancient study.

Mastery Academy of Chinese Metaphysics was established by Joey Yap to play the role of disseminating this Eastern knowledge to the modern world with the belief that this valuable knowledge should be accessible to anyone, anywhere.

Its goal is to enrich people's lives through accurate, professional teaching and practice of Chinese Metaphysics knowledge globally. It is the first academic institution of its kind in the world to adopt the tradition of Western institutions of higher learning - where students are encourage to explore, question and challenge themselves and to respect different fields and branches of study - with the appreciation and respect of classical ideas and applications that have stood the test of time.

The art and science of Chinese Metaphysics studies – be it Feng Shui, BaZi (Astrology), Mian Xiang (Face Reading), ZeRi (Date Selection) or Yi Jing – is no longer a field shrouded with mystery and superstition. In light of new technology, fresher interpretations and innovative methods as well as modern teaching tools like the Internet, interactive learning, e-learning and distance learning, anyone from virtually any corner of the globe, who is keen to master these disciplines can do so with ease and confidence under the guidance and support of the Academy.

It has indeed proven to be a center of educational excellence for thousands of students from over thirty countries across the world; many of whom have moved on to practice classical Chinese Metaphysics professionally in their home countries.

At the Academy, we believe in enriching people's lives by empowering their destinies through the disciplines of Chinese Metaphysics. Learning is not an option - it's a way of life!

MALAYSIA
19-3, The Boulevard, Mid Valley City, 59200 Kuala Lumpur, Malaysia
Tel : +603-2284 8080 | Fax : +603-2284 1218
Email   : info@masteryacademy.com
Website : www.masteryacademy.com

Australia, Austria, Canada, China, Croatia, Cyprus, Czech Republic, Denmark, France, Germany, Greece, Hungary, India, Italy, Kazakhstan, Malaysia, Netherlands (Holland), New Zealand, Philippines, Poland, Russian Federation, Singapore, Slovenia, South Africa, Switzerland, Turkey, U.S.A., Ukraine, United Kingdom

Mastery Academy around the world

JOEY YAP CONSULTING GROUP

Pioneering Metaphysics - Centric Personal Coaching and Corporate Consulting

The Joey Yap Consulting Group is the world's first specialised metaphysics consultation firm. Founded in 2002 by renown international Feng Shui and BaZi consultant, author and trainer Joey Yap, the Joey Yap Consulting Group is a pioneer in the provision of metaphysics-driven coaching and consultation services for individuals and corporations.

The Group's core consultation practice areas are Feng Shui and BaZi, which are complimented by ancillary services like Date Selection, Face Reading and Yi Jing Divination. The Group's team of highly-trained professional consultants are led by Principal Consultant Joey Yap. The Joey Yap Consulting Group is the firm of choice for corporate captains, entrepreneurs, celebrities and property developers when it comes to Feng Shui and BaZi-related advisory and knowledge.

Across Industries: Our Portfolio of Clients

Our diverse portfolio of both corporate and individual clients from all around the world bears testimony to our experience and capabilities.

Joey Yap Consulting Group is the firm of choice for many of Asia's leading multi-national corporations, listed entities, conglomerates and top-tier property developers when it comes to Feng Shui and corporate BaZi.

Our services also engaged by professionals, prominent business personalities, celebrities, high-profile politicians and people from all walks of life.

JOEY YAP CONSULTING GROUP

Name (Mr./Mrs./Ms.):_____

Contact Details

Tel:_____ Fax:_____

Mobile :_____

E-mail:_____

What Type of Consultation Are You Interested In?
- [ ] Feng Shui
- [ ] BaZi
- [ ] Date Selection
- [ ] Corporate Events

Please tick if applicable:
- [ ] Are you a Property Developer looking to engage Joey Yap Consulting Group?
- [ ] Are you a Property Investor looking for tailor-made packages to suit your investment requirements?

Please attach your name card here.

Thank you for completing this form. Please fax it back to us at:

Malaysia & the rest of the world
Fax : +603-2284 2213   Tel : +603-2284 1213

www.joeyyap.com

Feng Shui Consultations

For Residential Properties
- Initial Land/Property Assessment
- Residential Feng Shui Consultations
- Residential Land Selection
- End-to-End Residential Consultation

For Commercial Properties
- Initial Land/Property Assessment
- Commercial Feng Shui Consultations
- Commercial Land Selection
- End-to-End Commercial Consultation

For Property Developers
- End-to-End Consultation
- Post-Consultation Advisory Services
- Panel Feng Shui Consultant

For Property Investors
- Your Personal Feng Shui Consultant
- Tailor-Made Packages

For Memorial Parks & Burial Sites
- Yin House Feng Shui

BaZi Consultations

Personal Destiny Analysis
- Personal Destiny Analysis for Individuals
- Children's BaZi Analysis
- Family BaZi Analysis

Strategic Analysis for Corporate Organizations
- Corporate BaZi Consultations
- BaZi Analysis for Human Resource Management

Entrepreneurs & Business Owners
- BaZi Analysis for Entrepreneurs

Career Pursuits
- BaZi Career Analysis

Relationships
- Marriage and Compatibility Analysis
- Partnership Analysis

For Everyone
- Annual BaZi Forecast
- Your Personal BaZi Coach

Date Selection Consultations

- **Marriage Date Selection**
- **Caesarean Birth Date Selection**
- **House-Moving Date Selection**
- **Renovation & Groundbreaking Dates**
- **Signing of Contracts**
- **Official Openings**
- **Product Launches**

Corporate Events

Many reputable organizations and instituitions have worked closely with Joey Yap Consulting Group to build a synergistic business relationship by engaging our team of consultants, led by Joey Yap, as speakers at their corporate events.

We tailor our seminars and talks to suit the anticipated or pertinent group of audience. Be it department, subsidiary, your clients or even the entire corporation, we aim to fit your requirements in delivering the intended message(s).

Tel: +603-2284 1213   Email: consultation@joeyyap.com

CHINESE METAPHYSICS REFERENCE SERIES

The Chinese Metaphysics Reference Series is a collection of reference texts, source material, and educational textbooks to be used as supplementary guides by scholars, students, researchers, teachers and practitioners of Chinese Metaphysics.

These comprehensive and structured books provide fast, easy reference to aid in the study and practice of various Chinese Metaphysics subjects including Feng Shui, BaZi, Yi Jing, Zi Wei, Liu Ren, Ze Ri, Ta Yi, Qi Men and Mian Xiang.

The Chinese Metaphysics Compendium

At over 1,000 pages, the *Chinese Metaphysics Compendium* is a unique one-volume reference book that compiles all the formulas relating to Feng Shui, BaZi (Four Pillars of Destiny), Zi Wei (Purple Star Astrology), Yi Jing (I-Ching), Qi Men (Mystical Doorways), Ze Ri (Date Selection), Mian Xiang (Face Reading) and other sources of Chinese Metaphysics.

It is presented in the form of easy-to-read tables, diagrams and reference charts, all of which are compiled into one handy book. This first-of-its-kind compendium is presented in both English and the original Chinese, so that none of the meanings and contexts of the technical terminologies are lost.

The only essential and comprehensive reference on Chinese Metaphysics, and an absolute must-have for all students, scholars, and practitioners of Chinese Metaphysics.

The Ten Thousand Year Calendar (Pocket Edition)	The Ten Thousand Year Calendar	Dong Gong Date Selection	The Date Selection Compendium	Plum Blossoms Divination Reference Book	San Yuan Dragon Gate Eight Formations Water Method	Xuan Kong Da Gua Ten Thousand Year Calendar

Bazi Hour Pillar Useful Gods - Wood	Bazi Hour Pillar Useful Gods - Fire	Bazi Hour Pillar Useful Gods - Earth	Bazi Hour Pillar Useful Gods - Metal	Bazi Hour Pillar Useful Gods - Water	Xuan Kong Da Gua Structures Reference Book	Xuan Kong Da Gua 64 Gua Transformation Analysis

Bazi Structures and Structural Useful Gods - Wood	Bazi Structures and Structural Useful Gods - Fire	Bazi Structures and Structural Useful Gods - Earth	Bazi Structures and Structural Useful Gods - Metal	Bazi Structures and Structural Useful Gods - Water		Xuan Kong Purple White Script	Earth Study Discern Truth Second Edition

www.masteryacademy.com | +603 - 2284 8080

Joey Yap's BaZi Profiling System

Three Levels of BaZi Profiling (English & Chinese versions)

In BaZi Profiling, there are three levels that reflect three different stages of a person's personal nature and character structure.

Level 1 – The Day Master

The Day Master in a nutshell is the BASIC YOU. The inborn personality. It is your essential character. It answers the basic question "WHO AM I". There are ten basic personality profiles – the TEN Day Masters – each with its unique set of personality traits, likes and dislikes.

Level 2 – The Structure

The Structure is your behavior and attitude – in other words, how you use your personality. It expands on the Day Master (Level 1). The structure reveals your natural tendencies in life – are you more controlling, more of a creator, supporter, thinker or connector? Each of the Ten Day Masters express themselves differently through the FIVE Structures. Why do we do the things we do? Why do we like the things we like? – The answers are in our BaZi STRUCTURE.

Level 3 – The Profile

The Profile reveals your unique abilities and skills, the masks that you consciously and unconsciously "put on" as you approach and navigate the world. Your Profile speaks of your ROLES in life. There are TEN roles – or Ten BaZi Profiles. Everyone plays a different role.

What makes you happy and what does success mean to you is different to somebody else. Your sense of achievement and sense of purpose in life is unique to your Profile. Your Profile will reveal your unique style.

The path of least resistence to your success and wealth can only be accessed once you get into your "flow." Your BaZi Profile reveals how you can get FLOW. It will show you your patterns in work, relationship and social settings. Being AWARE of these patterns is your first step to positive Life Transformation.

www.baziprofiling.com

BaZi Collections

Leading Chinese Astrology Master Trainer Joey Yap makes it easy to learn how to unlock your Destiny through your BaZi with these books. BaZi or Four Pillars of Destiny is an ancient Chinese science which enables individuals to understand their personality, hidden talents and abilities as well as their luck cycle, simply by examining the information contained within their birth data.

Understand and appreciate more about this astoundingly accurate ancient Chinese Metaphysical science with this BaZi Collection.

Feng Shui Collection

Must-Haves for Property Analysis!

For homeowners, those looking to build their own home or even investors who are looking to apply Feng Shui to their homes, these series of books provides valuable information from the classical Feng Shui therioes and applications.

In his trademark straight-to-the-point manner, Joey shares with you the Feng Shui do's and dont's when it comes to finding a property with favorable Feng Shui, which is condusive for home living.

Stories & Lessons on Feng Shui Series

All in all, this series is a delightful chronicle of Joey's articles, thoughts and vast experience - as a professional Feng Shui consultant and instructor - that have been purposely refined, edited and expanded upon to make for a light-hearted, interesting yet educational read. And with Feng Shui, BaZi, Mian Xiang and Yi Jing all thrown into this one dish, there's something for everyone.

www.masteryacademy.com | +603 - 2284 8080

Continue Your Journey with Joey Yap Books in Feng Shui

Pure Feng Shui
Pure Feng Shui is Joey Yap's debut with an international publisher, CICO Books, and is a refreshing and elegant look at the intricacies of Classical Feng Shui – now compiled in a useful manner for modern-day readers. This book is a comprehensive introduction to all the important precepts and techniques of Feng Shui practice.

Your Aquarium Here
This book is the first in Fengshuilogy Series, a series of matter-in-fact and useful Feng Shui books designed for the person who wants to do a fuss-free Feng Shui.

Xuan Kong Flying Stars
This book is an essential introductory book to the subject of Xuan Kong Fei Xing, a well-known and popular system of Feng Shui. Learn 'tricks of the trade' and 'trade secrets' to enhance and maximize Qi in your home or office.

Walking the Dragons
Compiled in one book for the first time from Joey Yap's Feng Shui Mastery Excursion Series, the book highlights China's extensive, vibrant history with astute observations on the Feng Shui of important sites and places. Learn the landform formations of Yin Houses (tombs and burial places), as well as mountains, temples, castles, and villages.

The Art of Date Selection: Personal Date Selection
With the *Art of Date Selection: Personal Date Selection*, learn simple, practical methods you can employ to select not just good dates, but personalized good dates. Whether it's a personal activity such as a marriage or professional endeavor such as launching a business, signing a contract or even acquiring assets, this book will show you how to pick the good dates and tailor them to suit the activity in question, as well as avoid the negative ones too!

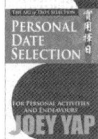

www.masteryacademy.com | +603 - 2284 8080

Face Reading Collection

Discover Face Reding (English & Chinese versions)

This is a comprehensive book on all areas of Face Reading, covering some of the most important facial features, including the forehead, mouth, ears and even philtrum above your lips. This book eill help you analyse not just your Destiny but help you achieve your full potential and achieve life fulfillment.

Joey Yap's Art of Face Reading

The Art of Face Reading is Joey Yap's second effort with CICO Books, and takes a lighter, more practical approach to Face Reading. This book does not so much focus on the individual features as it does on reading the entire face. It is about identifying common personality types and characters.

Easy Guide on Face Reading (English & Chinese versions)

The Face Reading Essentials series of books comprises 5 individual books on the key features of the face – Eyes, Eyebrows, Ears, Nose, and Mouth. Each book provides a detailed illustration and a simple yet descriptive explanation on the individual types of the features.

The books are equally useful and effective for beginners, enthusiasts, and the curious. The series is designed to enable people who are new to Face Reading to make the most of first impressions and learn to apply Face Reading skills to understand the personality and character of friends, family, co-workers, and even business associates.

Annual Releases
2011 Annual Outlook & Tong Shu

| Chinese Astrology for 2011 | Feng Shui for 2011 | Tong Shu Desktop Calendar 2011 | Professional Tong Shu Diary 2011 | Tong Shu Monthly Planner 2011 | Weekly Tong Shu Diary 2011 |

www.masteryacademy.com | +603 - 2284 8080

Educational Tools and Software

Xuan Kong Flying Stars Feng Shui Software
The Essential Application for Enthusiasts and Professionals

The Xuan Kong Flying Stars Feng Shui Software will assist you in the practice of Xuan Kong Feng Shui with minimum fuss and maximum effectiveness. Superimpose the Flying Stars charts over your house plans (or those of your clients) to clearly demarcate the 9 Palaces. Use it to help you create fast and sophisticated chart drawings and presentations, as well as to assist professional practitioners in the report-writing process before presenting the final reports for your clients. Students can use it to practice their Xuan Kong Feng Shui skills and knowledge, and it can even be used by designers and architects!

BaZi Ming Pan Software Version 2.0
Professional Four Pillars Calculator for Destiny Analysis

The BaZi Ming Pan Version 2.0 Professional Four Pillars Calculator for Destiny Analysis is the most technically advanced software of its kind in the world today. It allows even those without any knowledge of BaZi to generate their own BaZi Charts, and provides virtually every detail required to undertake a comprehensive Destiny Analysis.

This Professional Four Pillars Calculator allows you to even undertake a day-to-day analysis of your Destiny. What's more, all BaZi Charts generated by this software are fully printable and configurable! Designed for both enthusiasts and professional practitioners, this state-of-the-art software blends details with simplicity, and is capable of generating 4 different types of BaZi charts: **BaZi Professional Charts, BaZi Annual Analysis Charts, BaZi Pillar Analysis Charts and BaZi Family Relationship Charts.**

Joey Yap Feng Shui Template Set

Directions are the cornerstone of any successful Feng Shui audit or application. The **Joey Yap Feng Shui Template Set** is a set of three templates to simplify the process of taking directions and determining locations and positions, whether it's for a building, a house, or an open area such as a plot of land, all with just a floor plan or area map.

The Set comprises 3 basic templates: The Basic Feng Shui Template, 8 Mansions Feng Shui Template, and the Flying Stars Feng Shui Template.

Mini Feng Shui Compass

The Mini Feng Shui Compass is a self-aligning compass that is not only light at 100gms but also built sturdily to ensure it will be convenient to use anywhere. The rings on the Mini Feng Shui Compass are bi-lingual and incorporate the 24 Mountain Rings that is used in your traditional Luo Pan.

The comprehensive booklet included will guide you in applying the 24 Mountain Directions on your Mini Feng Shui Compass effectively and the 8 Mansions Feng Shui to locate the most auspicious locations within your home, office and surroundings. You can also use the Mini Feng Shui Compass when measuring the direction of your property for the purpose of applying Flying Stars Feng Shui.

Educational Tools and Software

Xuan Kong Vol.1
An Advanced Feng Shui Home Study Course

Learn the Xuan Kong Flying Star Feng Shui system in just 20 lessons! Joey Yap's specialised notes and course work have been written to enable distance learning without compromising on the breadth or quality of the syllabus. Learn at your own pace with the same material students in a live class would use. The most comprehensive distance learning course on Xuan Kong Flying Star Feng Shui in the market. Xuan Kong Flying Star Vol.1 comes complete with a special binder for all your course notes.

Feng Shui for Period 8 - (DVD)

Don't miss the Feng Shui Event of the next 20 years! Catch Joey Yap LIVE and find out just what Period 8 is all about. This DVD boxed set zips you through the fundamentals of Feng Shui and the impact of this important change in the Feng Shui calendar. Joey's entertaining, conversational style walks you through the key changes that Period 8 will bring and how to tap into Wealth Qi and Good Feng Shui for the next 20 years.

Xuan Kong Flying Stars Beginners Workshop - (DVD)

Take a front row seat in Joey Yap's Xuan Kong Flying Stars workshop with this unique LIVE RECORDING of Joey Yap's Xuan Kong Flying Stars Feng Shui workshop, attended by over 500 people. This DVD program provides an effective and quick introduction of Xuan Kong Feng Shui essentials for those who are just starting out in their study of classical Feng Shui. Learn to plot your own Flying Star chart in just 3 hours. Learn 'trade secret' methods, remedies and cures for Flying Stars Feng Shui. This boxed set contains 3 DVDs and 1 workbook with notes and charts for reference.

BaZi Four Pillars of Destiny Beginners Workshop - (DVD)

Ever wondered what Destiny has in store for you? Or curious to know how you can learn more about your personality and inner talents? BaZi or Four Pillars of Destiny is an ancient Chinese science that enables us to understand a person's hidden talent, inner potential, personality, health and wealth luck from just their birth data. This specially compiled DVD set of Joey Yap's BaZi Beginners Workshop provides a thorough and comprehensive introduction to BaZi. Learn how to read your own chart and understand your own luck cycle. This boxed set contains 3 DVDs and 1 workbook with notes and reference charts.

www.masteryacademy.com | +603 - 2284 8080

DVD Series

Joey Yap's Face Reading Revealed DVD Series
Mian Xiang, the Chinese art of Face Reading, is an ancient form of physiognomy and entails the use of the face and facial characteristics to evaluate key aspects of a person's life, luck and destiny. In his Face Reading DVDs series, Joey Yap shows you how the facial features reveal a wealth of information about a person's luck, destiny and personality.

Mian Xiang also tell us the talents, quirks and personality of an individual. Do you know that just by looking at a person's face, you can ascertain his or her health, wealth, relationships and career? Let Joey Yap show you how the 12 Palaces can be utilised to reveal a person's inner talents, characteristics and much more.

Feng Shui for Homebuyers DVD Series
In these DVDs, you will also learn how to identify properties with good Feng Shui features that will help you promote a fulfilling life and achieve your full potential. Discover how to avoid properties with negative Feng Shui that can bring about detrimental effects to your health, wealth and relationships.

Joey will also elaborate on how to fix the various aspects of your home that may have an impact on the Feng Shui of your property and give pointers on how to tap into the positive energies to support your goals.

Discover Feng Shui with Joey Yap: Set of 4 DVDs
Informative and entertaining, classical Feng Shui comes alive in *Discover Feng Shui with Joey Yap!*

You have the questions. Now let Joey personally answer them in this 4-set DVD compilation! Learn how to ensure the viability of your residence or workplace, Feng Shui-wise, without having to convert it into a Chinese antiques' shop. Classical Feng Shui is about harnessing the natural power of your environment to improve quality of life. It's a systematic and subtle metaphysical science.

Walking the Dragons with Joey Yap (The TV Series)
This DVD set features eight episodes, covering various landform Feng Shui analyses and applications from Joey Yap as he and his co-hosts travel through China. It includes case studies of both modern and historical sites with a focus on Yin House (burial places) Feng Shui and the tombs of the Qing Dynasty emperors.

The series was partly filmed on-location in mainland China, and the state of Selangor, Malaysia.

Home Study Courses

Gain Valuable Knowledge from the Comfort of Your Home

Now, armed with your trusty computer or laptop and Internet access, knowledge of Chinese Metaphysics is just a click away!

3 easy steps to activate your Home Study Course:

Step 1: Go to the URL as indicated on the Activation Card, and key in your Activation Code
Step 2: At the Registration page, fill in the details accordingly to enable us to generate your Student Identification (Student ID).
Step 3: Upon successful registration, you may begin your lessons immediately.

Joey Yap's Feng Shui Mastery HomeStudy Course

Module 1: **Empowering Your Home**
Module 2: **Master Practitioner Program**

Learn how easy it is to harness the power of the environment to promote health, wealth and prosperity in your life. The knowledge and applications of Feng Shui will no more be a mystery but a valuable tool you can master on your own.

Joey Yap's BaZi Mastery HomeStudy Course

Module 1: **Mapping Your Life**
Module 2: **Mastering Your Future**

Discover your path of least resistance to success with insights about your personality and capabilities, and what strengths you can tap on to maximize your potential for success and happiness by mastering BaZi (Chinese Astrology). This course will teach you all the essentials you need to interpret a BaZi chart and more.

Joey Yap's Mian Xiang Mastery HomeStudy Course

Module 1: **Face Reading**
Module 2: **Advanced Face Reading**

A face can reveal so much about a person. Now, you can learn the art and science of Mian Xiang (Chinese Face Reading) to understand a person's character based on his or her facial features with ease and confidence.

www.masteryacademy.com | +603 - 2284 8080

Feng Shui Mastery™
LIVE COURSES (MODULES ONE TO FOUR)

The Feng Shui Mastery™ comprises Feng Shui Mastery Modules 1, 2, 3 and 4. It starts off with a foundation program up to the advanced practitioner level. It is a thorough, comprehensive program that covers important theories from various classical Feng Shui systems including Ba Zhai, San Yuan, San He, and Xuan Kong.

Module One: Beginners Course **Module Two:** Practitioners Course **Module Three:** Advanced Practitioners Course **Module Four:** Master Course

BaZi Mastery™
LIVE COURSES (MODULES ONE TO FOUR)

The BaZi Mastery™ consists of BaZi Mastery Modules 1, 2, 3 and 4. In Modules 1 and 2, students will receive a thorough introduction to BaZi, along with an intensive understanding of BaZi principles and the requisite skills to practice it with accuracy and precision. This will prepare them, and serious Feng Shui practitioners, for a more advanced levels and fine-tune their application skills in Modules 3 and 4.

Module One: Intensive Foundation Course **Module Two:** Practitioners Course **Module Three:** Advanced Practitioners Course **Module Four:** Master Course in BaZi

XUAN KONG MASTERY™
LIVE COURSES (MODULES ONE TO THREE)
*Advanced Courses For Master Practitioners

The Xuan Kong Mastery™ comprises Xuan Kong Mastery Modules 1, 2A, 2B and 3. It is a sophisticated branch of Feng Shui replete with many techniques and formulae, enabling practitioners to evaluate Feng Shui on a more thorough and in-depth basis. The study of Xuan Kong encompasses numerology, symbology and science of the Ba Gua along with the mathematics of time.

Module One: Advanced Foundation Course **Module Two A:** Advanced Xuan Kong Methodologies **Module Two B:** Purple White **Module Three:** Advanced Xuan Kong Da Gua

www.masteryacademy.com | +603 - 2284 8080

Mian Xiang Mastery™
LIVE COURSES (MODULES ONE AND TWO)

The Mian Xiang Mastery™ comprises of Mian Xiang Mastery Modules 1 and 2 to allow students to learn this ancient art in a thorough, detailed manner. Each module has a carefully-developed syllabus that allows students to get acquainted with the fundamentals of Mian Xiang before moving on to the more intricate theories and principles that will enable them to practice Mian Xiang with greater depth and complexity.

 **Module One:** Basic Face Reading

 **Module Two:** Practical Face Reading

 # Yi Jing Mastery™
LIVE COURSES (MODULES ONE AND TWO)

The Yi Jing Mastery™ comprises Modules 1 and 2. Both Modules aim to give casual and serious Yi Jing enthusiasts a serious insight into one of the most important philosophical treatises in ancient Chinese thought. Yi Jing uses sophisticated formulas and calculations to derive the answers to questions we pose. It is a science of divination, and in our classes there is a heavy emphasis on the scientific aspect of it. It bears no religious or superstitious affiliation.

 **Module One:** Traditional Yi Jing

 **Module Two:** Plum Blossom Numerology

 # Ze Ri Mastery™
LIVE COURSES (MODULES ONE AND TWO)

The ZeRi Mastery™ consists of ZeRi Mastery Modules 1 and 2. This program provides students with a thorough introduction to the art of Date Selection both for Personal and Feng Shui purposes. Our ZeRi Mastery™ aims to provide a thorough and comprehensive program on the art of Date Selection, covering everything from Personal and Feng Shui Date Selection to Xuan Kong Da Gua Date Selection.

 **Module One:** Personal and Feng Shui Date Selection

 **Module Two:** Xuan Kong Da Gua Date Selection

www.masteryacademy.com | +603 - 2284 8080

Feng Shui for Life

This is an entry-level five-day course designed for the Feng Shui beginner to learn the application of practical Feng Shui in day-to-day living. Lessons include quick tips on analyzing the BaZi chart, simple Feng Shui solutions for the home, basic Date Selection, useful Face Reading techniques and practical Water formulas. A great introduction course on Chinese Metaphysics studies for beginners.

Joey Yap's
Design Your Destiny

This is a three-day life transformation program designed to inspire awareness and action for you to create a better quality of life. It introduces the DRT™ (Decision Referential Technology) method, which utilizes the BaZi Personality Profiling system to determine the right version of you, and serves as a tool to help you make better decisions and achieve a better life in the least resistant way possible based on your Personality Profile Type.

Walk the Mountains! Learn Feng Shui in a Practical and Hands-on Program

Feng Shui Mastery Excursion™

Learn landform (Luan Tou) Feng Shui by walking the mountains and chasing the Dragon's vein in China. This Program takes the students in a study tour to examine notable Feng Shui landmarks, mountains, hills, valleys, ancient palaces, famous mansions, houses and tombs in China. The Excursion is a 'practical' hands-on course where students are shown to perform readings using the formulas they've learnt and to recognize and read Feng Shui Landform (Luan Tou) formations.

Read about China Excursion here:
http://www.fengshuiexcursion.com

Mastery Academy courses are conducted around the world. Find out when will Joey Yap be in your area by visiting **www.masteryacademy.com** or call our office at **+603-2284 8080**.

www.masteryacademy.com | +603 - 2284 8080